Writing to Heal

Jacqui Malpass

WRITING TO HEAL

HEAL YOUR LIFE THROUGH JOURNALING AND CREATIVE LIFE WRITING

JACQUI MALPASS

WRITING TO HEAL

Just wanted to let you know that I started reading your book this morning and was instantly hooked. I got as far as you bit on Prof James Pennebaker, found a book to write in and have written 7 pages on the most traumatic experience in my life, cried buckets but loved getting it down on paper and feel so much better with it being out and there's so many pages to add over the next 4 days (in between the Rugby of course)! Inspirational Jacqui - congratulations and thank you, perfect timing - looking forward to reading the rest of the book as well as writing.

….this bit comes from my soul - your book is, I feel going to save my life, not from death but from disillusionment - a life of disillusionment - can you imagine! I've been facing that for a while and today you gave me the path out of that, the path I've been looking in the long grass for! For the first time in 2 years I sit here now with a jewel of excitement in my belly.

LEGAL NOTICES

No part of this publication may be reproduced or transmitted in any material form (including photocopying or storing it in any medium by electronic means) without the written permission of the author.

The purpose of this book is to educate, entertain and provide information on the subject matter covered. All attempts have been made to verify information at the time of this publication and the author does not assume any responsibility for errors, omissions or other interpretations of the subject matter. The purchaser or reader of this book assumes responsibility for the use of this material and information. The author assumes no responsibility or liability on the behalf of any purchaser or reader of this book.

Copyright © 2013 Jacqui Malpass
All rights reserved.

ISBN-13: 978-1481101691
ISBN-10: 1481101692

DEDICATION

Writing to heal is dedicated to mum, dad, Richard and Ferdy dog. To all of the people I meet randomly, thank you for having faith and putting pen to paper.

TABLE OF CONTENTS

Introduction	1
My Story	7
Writing to Heal	15
How to use this book	25
Stuff that gets in the way	35
Writing from the heart	53
In the writers rucksack	57
Starting to write	63
Timelines	79
All about me	87
Getting from values to vision	101
Writing exercises	119
Reflecting	129
Reflection exercises	137
Reflecting through creative writing	163
Telling tales	185
Other stories, poems & prose	197
Resources	207
About the author	211

Writing to Heal

INTRODUCTION

"If you can journal, you can write, if you can write, you can create short stories and if you can produce short stories, you can join them together and you can write a book. And if you can do just one part of this you can heal."

Getting started is the hardest part, so let's just start.

At the Masquerade ball of life we dance out our stories. You don't know me or my stories, we share our dances and make guesses about who each other is and what lies behind the social mask.

The fun of the ball is wearing masks and costumes to protect us from others' perceptions, to shield our identity and to become someone else; the someone else you want the world to know and see, the mask that you wear sharply contrasting with the you that lurks inside.

We land in this world naked without words to define us or masks to hide behind, we simply trust that we will be taken care of and loved. From those innocent first moments when no one tells us we can't dance that way, our minds drink in what is possible. Then we grow up, discover, and learn that things are not possible and that often there is another tune that we must dance to.

As we dance, the music changes, the steps become more difficult, a new partner may step in, the heady irresistible whirl of life moves us forward and then too soon the ball is over. When we look back to reflect on the steps we took, the costume that we wore or the partner we danced with, there is a realisation that it's too late; the band has packed up and gone home.

The party can go on.

When faced with the impossible we can break the rules or buckle under. For some, no matter what life throws at them, they plough on regardless, sometimes taking small steps and occasionally giant leaps. They keep moving forward in their dance of life. Their expectation is if it is possible in the world, it is possible for me.

The rest feel abandoned.

The dance of self-transformation is to lose your entire being to the flow of your pen, unstructured, improvised and cascading over the paper, metamorphosing the Masquerade ball into an Argentine Tango to breathe life, love, and happiness back into your life.

Imagine taking your writing onto the dance floor, where you take the lead role and put yourself back in control, moving in response to the music and letting your spirit move you.

I am fascinated by the power of words, self-reflection and passionate about encouraging others to write, to find their voices through the written word, to shape their lives around their words and to use their words to set them free.

Writing to Heal takes you on a journey that asks you to first pick up your pen and write in a journal, to then reflect on what you have written and rewrite it with positive intention so that you change the story.

As you change the way in which you view life and your story, your life will change. Add in the dimension of creative life writing, through short stories, prose, or poems, and suddenly you are on an adventure where you are in control of your destiny. You can now decide what happens to the characters and what the outcome of the tale might be.

For anyone who has ever been fed up of being on the end of someone else's stuff, you can turn the tables in your writing and take them on an imaginary dance.

Your tales can be dark or light, funny and bright, sad and poignant, bold and mad, but most of all your journaling and writing is yours to own and craft.

Your story is your journey.

Open your heart and let it flow, who knows where your story will go?

Once you start to journal, write, and reflect, you may feel inspired to take your writing further and create a book of your life.

Instead of being afraid to write about you and your life, you can now meld it into a work of fiction. No one will ever know which is fact or fiction, only you. No one will be offended or worried that you may expose them. Your family, friends, and readers may know that you have drawn your inspiration from life, but they need never know which bits are true.

Start today with a journal. In a week start reflecting on what you have written and, when you are ready, start crafting some wicked life stories, poems, or prose. The book can come later.

You and I share a few things in common. I knew I had a story and it was time to let go and heal, I just couldn't figure out how to write it, couldn't decide if I wanted to share it. I was scared to expose myself, not to others but to myself, and I didn't know where to start.

I just started. Writing in my journal opened up old wounds which needed healing. I became emotional, angry and wanted to give up.

I set out to research my story from my own memory, professional knowledge and through books (mostly psychology), and also to learn the craft of writing and how to apply it to my writing for both memoir and novel.

In doing all of this work, over many years, I have been able to heal, forgive and learn to love myself.

In this book I teach you what I know about journaling, reflection, and change.

If you are at a point in your life where you feel that you need to let go of the past, so that you can step into a brighter future, writing in your journal will help you.

I won't lie; none of my writing has been easy. I have cried and cried as I have journaled. Equally I have screamed with hysterical laughter when I have read my creative life stories and plotted the demise of others who I felt had hurt me.

When I wrote, I didn't expect to reach into the pit of hell, I thought I was ok to tackle the BIG subject - me. I wasn't and I sunk into a vipers nest, resting whilst their poison spread. With heavy heart and all of my tears shed for what was, I picked myself up and carried on to write a happier future. As I continued to write, the pain in my chest eased and the path ahead began to shine. I felt more at peace with myself.

I have one hope for this book, that it will help you to get off your bum and embrace the cathartic process of writing and begin to heal old wounds.

What I ask is that you trust yourself. You don't have to publish your journal, it is enough that you put pen to paper and use this as a way to discover who you are, why you do what you do or did and heal.

Remember, everything that you need to heal yourself is right inside you.

Writing to Heal

MY STORY

"The unexamined life is not worth living."
Socrates, in Plato, Dialogues, Apology. Greek philosopher in Athens (469 BC - 399 BC)

You ask about turning points, of crossroads, forks in the road and journeys. I ask you, who hasn't encountered an unexpected bend, a twist or turn they weren't anticipating? Every day the master plan, the route through life continues exactly as it should and yet we face it with fear, disappointment, and anger. We get on the bus and sit helplessly as it drives us, we think, in the wrong direction.

When I was expelled from school, I called my dad at work, expecting the usual telling off. The sting of his words, 'are you mental or what?' wrenched my heart. I held back the tears and swallowed hard, he simply put the phone down on me. Dad had a philosophy on life; you could do whatever you liked as long as you weren't caught. And caught I duly was. I was certainly my fathers' daughter; a rebel. I think he quite liked it, but equally hated the fuss when he had to deal with my games. Mental, no, naughty, yes, bored, yes, ignored, yes. No one talked or looked at me that week, whilst I, slightly unconcerned, relished my newfound freedom. A few days later I found myself on a farm with the Moonies.

The farm was beautiful, though disturbingly filled with aliens and other waifs looking just like me, grey smiles glued to pasty faces. Great food, fresh from the fields; brightly coloured vegetables contrasted against the dull people sitting around me. I wondered how I could escape. Cocooned in my bunk bed, an overactive fertile mind retraced my steps, out through the door, over the muddy tractor tracks into the lane, but which way next? If I ran, surely they would know and capture me, then what?

The next two days were hell on earth, trapped once more in the classroom, with no unescorted time to myself, Richard, my yellow haired new best friend by my side, lectures from early in the morning to late at night interspersed with food. This was worse than school! The drone of the lecturer's voice kept sending me into a lull, tales of Christ, and his reincarnation irking me. As my mind drifted in and out of the room I was appalled to hear that Reverend Sun Myung Moon was indeed the second coming of Christ. So that's what we were here for, the aliens wanted to turn us into moon children! My heightened senses told me I must escape.

These people were nuts and I wanted to go home to face my punishment. My dad was right, I was mental.

Back in Cardiff, they let me go. I didn't fit.

I turned a corner and headed straight back into education via night school and a job in a factory.

Fast forward to my forties. My bus, I thought, had started to move in the wrong direction.

I had had a stellar career, rising from clerk in the tax office to a well-respected business marketing manager for one of the UK's top computer companies, with a shiny black BMW, and very nice salary.

I came to loathe this company, decided to leave my shiny BMW and jumped into my girl racer MG and sped back to Wales to what I had thought would be a fresh start.

Within a few short months the company that I had joined changed hands. I wasn't part of the blueprint, I was let go, and once again I didn't fit.

The bus rumbled on over rocky ground, my life juddered, I fell apart, and my confidence was crushed. I turned and looked out of the back window. In the distance, a disjointed childhood, constant moving, fighting parents, all the battles I had fought to survive in a man's world, overachievement, an MBA, failed relationships and so much more I couldn't face. I felt a failure and I pondered who would want me now?

All around me, trappings of success, big house and stuff. I wondered how I came to have all of this, to be a part of this strange game. It didn't matter, I needed to keep it. 18 months of hard slog later, clients who didn't pay on time or at all and an unemployed drunk in my bed, the bus juddered to a halt, a hard smack of reality pushed me into a yet another job.

For 2 more years I painted a smile on my face as I pushed the heavy factory doors open, shone my glitter on the day, did what I do, returning home to pity.

For years I had watched my mother helpless and in denial whilst my father drank. My father, dying from his addiction, had my mother to wipe his arse, feed and dress him. I have had to sit and watch helplessly as two people that I love played out their awful lives. And then I had the pleasure of watching my partner do the same.

Every day I dragged myself out of bed to go work, I wanted more from my life but I was caught in a limbo land where I couldn't move. I was trapped, caught in the spider's web and watching horrified as life passed me by.

One night his hands closed around my throat, I knew in that moment that I would rather be dead than spend another moment with him. He squeezed, took the breath from me, I closed my eyes and waited for the blows. In those moments I felt what it would be like to be beaten beyond recognition. I closed my eyes and waited. His swollen red hand left my throat, defeated he walked away. Someone had saved me. I sucked in air, and the menace was gone. I walked slowly up the stairs to my bedroom and the sanctuary that I would come to love.

In there I wrote and reflected, writing becoming my saviour and my passion.

It was summertime when my office door opened, that day I knew the clip clop of HR heels were for me. The bus to hell had come back for me; the new MD didn't like me. I didn't fit, and he sent me on my way, to join the other directors on the unemployment line. Another fork in the road.

The bus skidded around a massive corner; I sped away from the relationship, house, and the shackles towards a different world.

The driver, not content to deliver me safely to my destination, ripped through the countryside, over yet more obstacles, forcing me to face each bump. I didn't want to, I wanted calm.

I buried my head in writing, it had saved me once before. I was convinced it would again.

Relentlessly, day after day, I wrote about my life. When one day I stood back to consider what I had written, great ugly boulders of shame raged down on me. Standing amongst broken rocks, unable to cope, I cried hot tears for what I had done to myself. The abused became the self-abuser. But, at last, clarity.

The bus stopped, the driver let me off. The journey wasn't over and almost certainly there will be bumpy times ahead, but he assures me that in facing my darkest fears, acknowledging that what I was, is not who I am, the road ahead, surrounded by cherished friends and family and with pen in my hand, I knew it would get easier.

There comes a time in many people's lives when the life we are living no longer makes any sense, we feel stuck and fearful of facing our demons. Unknown and unseen monsters tear away at us. We unwittingly shape our lives, putting on a face for our public and all the while we live in constant terror that one day someone will unearth our secrets and show us for the frauds we really are.

When that time comes we search blindly, looking for answers about who we are in the strangest places, when in reality the search needs to move inwards, where all of the answers reside.

In taking the brave step to examine who we are and the things we have done or had done to us, we run the risk of crashing. When our bus careers over the precipice and we hit the bottom of the canyon there is only one way out and that is to take control and write ourselves into a new adventure, where we are the heroines (or heroes) and can control our outcomes.

Through writing, reflection, and creativity, it can all be pulled into perspective.

Writing to Heal

What I want to offer anyone who wonders what next? Put pen to paper, see what emerges, reflect, and learn a new way of writing the next part of your journey.

Writing is cathartic and when your soul is laid bare, you can either lie down and die or you can recognise who you are and fight back.

Writing won't solve anyone's issues but it will help to shine a light and in the process enable painful memories to be uncovered, written about, and for healing to take place.

I work on the premise that we are all perfectly imperfect (to steal a title from Lee Woodruff) and that we are the best judges of how to heal ourselves, although we may not know it in our darker moments.

At no time do I suggest that anyone's life needs fixing or gluing back together, just that we all have a personal choice about what we do next.

What I ask is that the writer trusts her or himself.

Jacqui Malpass

WRITING TO HEAL

"The act of putting pen to paper encourages pause for thought, this in turn makes us think more deeply about life, which helps us regain our equilibrium." Norbet Platt

What is Writing to Heal?

Writing is cathartic and healing; you will only know this for certain if you actually do it. Thankfully more and more research is coming to the fore which proves this.

Keeping a diary/journal can be traced back centuries; the earliest I can remember was that of Samuel Pepys, which was part of my school life. Another notable one, The Diary of a Young Girl by Anne Frank, tells of life in the German occupation. Anais Nin, another famous diarist, provided us with a 'fictional' view into her 'torturous' life. And of course, on a much lighter note, Bridget Jones.

WHAT IS THERAPEUTIC WRITING?

Writing is incredibly healing, the very act of writing releases tension and allows your subconscious thoughts to flow and, upon reflection, you begin to see sense, patterns, and ways through your problems.

Research into therapeutic writing, though sparse, shows that it deserves its place in modern psychology, with distinguished people such as Prof. James Pennebaker who, over 30 years ago, conducted research with his students. His research showed that those that undertook the brief trauma recall exercises demonstrated an increase in personal wellbeing.

He instructed his students to write:-

For the next 4 days, I would like you to write your very deepest thoughts and feelings about the most traumatic experience of your entire life or an extremely important emotional issue that has affected you and your life. In your writing, I'd like you to really let go and explore your deepest emotions and thoughts. You might tie your topic to your relationships with others, including parents, lovers, friends, or relatives; to your past, your present or your future; or to who you have been, who you would like to be or who you are now. You may write about the same general issues or experiences on all days of writing or about different topics each day. All of your writing will be completely confidential.

Don't worry about spelling, grammar or sentence structure. The only rule is that once you begin writing, you continue until the time is up.

Other notable researchers are Gillie Bolton in the UK and Kathleen Adams in US who founded The Therapeutic Writing Institute. Both are well worth looking up.

Unlike our famous diarists, many of us do not want the world to know our raw feelings and thoughts. There are many reasons that we would want to keep these feelings to ourselves, not least because they are private, often confused and other people may interpret what we say in a way in which we didn't intend.

If you are planning to write a book or penning your memoirs, journaling is the place to start.

WHAT IS JOURNALING?

A journal is a written record of your thoughts, feelings, experiences, and observations. You can write in your journal daily, or only when you feel the urge. Journaling is then the act of keeping, writing, reflecting and making personal change through the art of keeping a journal.

WHY JOURNAL?

Writing in a journal is such a fantastic and cathartic way of getting lots of stuff out in private. We are sometimes plagued with thoughts and emotions we don't understand, nor do we want to tell anyone about.

The main reason you are keeping a journal is that you want to be able to freely express and be able to say exactly what you want and through reflection seek to make meaning, change aspects of your life, and live in better harmony with yourself.

BENEFITS OF JOURNALING

Because your journal is private you can:-

- Express your feelings and thoughts in an uninhibited way.
- Clarify goals before acting.
- Release unhelpful thoughts and learn to let go.
- Gain a sense of perspective and control.
- Store and analyse your dreams.
- Catalyst for change and creativity.
- A source for your stories and your memoirs.

You will start to:-

- Understand who you are, what you want and how to get it.
- Find new ways to tackle old behaviours, issues or problems.
- Unwind and relax.
- Communicate with others better.
- Create positive intentions and affirmations.

Discover a pathway to self-awareness which provides insights, upon which you can act and create change.

Find creative solutions to problems and challenges.

Discover memories.

Let me ask you:-

Do you feel stuck and unable to move on?

Have you tried every personal development course available, but still feel no further forward?

Have you ever wanted to write your life story or memoir, but stopped, staring blankly at the page in front of you? Full of doubts you put your pen away.

When you do write, do you fill up with emotion and can't move on?

What if you could take the bold step of exploring you and your life and could discover how to make changes through writing and reflection? Would you be tempted?

What if you could get your story out, heal your wounds, be in control and confident? Would you want to take that step?

HOW TO JOURNAL

There are no rules. You need a pen and some paper, the right environment and the desire to let go and write. Of course it is often not that simple, which is where this book comes in to inspire and motivate you.

WHAT IS CREATIVE LIFE WRITING?

Creative life writing is where you take any of your journal entries and turn them into stories. You meld fact with fiction and, most importantly, the story goes the way you want it to. I have such fun with this. When someone or something upsets me, I write a story and in no time at all I am laughing.

WHY CREATIVE WRITING?

In all stories there are a number of elements, just like your life:-

- Your central character
- Other players
- A beginning, middle, and end
- A conflict
- A plot

In your stories you can take things from real life and take them in any direction and I guarantee it is extremely cathartic and fun.

HOW TO WRITE CREATIVELY

First of all, believe that you can. By using your journal as a source of your stories, you have your inspiration, and then allow your imagination to take over. I provide ideas in a later chapter.

WHAT IS MEMOIR?

The Merriam-Webster Dictionary defines memoir as *"a narrative composed from personal experience"*. It is often confused with autobiography which is described beautifully by Gore Vidal *"A memoir is how one remembers one's own life, while an autobiography is history, requiring research, dates, facts double-checked."*

For me memoir is a slice of life, my life and told just as I want to. I wanted to write a novel, but couldn't as I needed to get my stuff out of the way, in writing a short memoir, I was able to unlock my creativity.

If writing your memoir is a dream, Writing to Heal will help you to get to a point where you will be able to. If you want to write a novel and feel stuck, maybe you need to do what I did, journal, reflect, write creative life stories and then a memoir. It is all material for all of your writing.

WHY WRITE YOUR MEMOIR?

There are many reasons to write your memoir, in the context of this book, it would be to release the demons and to move from what was to be what is and can be.

Memoir is also a wonderful way to connect to the hearts of others and to leave behind a trace of you.

IS THERE A BOOK IN YOU?

Many times when you start to write in your journal and subsequently move on to write stories a desire to share more is awakened. You can see opportunities to help other people and that's when you start to ask, should I write a book?

When you have written your book, the next question is often - should I publish my book? That is a decision that only you can take. You can of course use self-publishing to produce a book just for you or your family or you can unleash your book on the world.

HOW TO WRITE YOUR MEMOIR

How to get your memoir written is certainly a subject for another book. My simple suggestion is that you use your journal to capture your memories and try your hand at creative life writing first. Hold that desire in your intention, consider which slice of life and start collecting together stories that might make up your memoir.

TO TELL THE TRUTH OR NOT

There are many versions of the truth, yours, theirs, and the 'real' truth. We selectively and unconsciously remember things in different ways. Can you really remember what the weather was like when you played rounders at 12? Of course not, but that is trivial.

The truth is, however, your truth. Your journaling and your subsequent stories are all about you.

The secrets which you share must come from your perspective. Imagine if, through journaling and writing about how you feel you were able to give birth to a new relationship with yourself or a person who has possibly upset you?

What if you were able to tell 'your' truth and lay to rest some of the feelings that were attached to that time of your life? Writing is cathartic, I keep saying it and it's true, you will find this to be true as you gain more confidence with your pen.

Be patient as you write, you may stall, stumble over the truth, feel a rush of emotion, and not want to go on. When you stall, be kind to yourself, take some time out, then come back, try an exercise, reflect. I highly recommend that, if you know that you will get emotional, you have some kind of ritual to help you.

Whether you write about darkness or light, the most important thing is you write, reflect and make the choice to change your life to be just what you want it to be.

HOW TO GET THE MOST OUT OF WRITING TO HEAL

Writing to Heal is designed to get you journaling, writing, reflecting, and making changes. When you are doing exercises, you will no longer be a reader; you will become an active journaler and writer. I encourage you to really let go and just write.

Of course, working on the exercises will slow down your reading time; that is intentional, this whole book is designed to awaken your creativity, build your confidence, and inspire you to write. Just dip in and out as you feel. I rarely read books in a linear fashion. Just open a page and go with the flow.

I encourage you to take an active part in your journaling and writing journey. Thinking about doing is not the same as creating some action and actually getting down to it.

Once you have started, you will not want to stop. Once you have learned how to journal, I guarantee you cannot unlearn it. Getting great aha moments, and clarity is addictive. It is wonderfully enabling, to discover that everything you ever needed is inside you.

Jacqui Malpass

Writing to Heal

HOW TO USE THIS BOOK

"There is no greater agony than bearing an untold story inside you." Maya Angelou

How to use this book, so that it works for you

This is a guide for you to use in the best way that suits you. We all work in different ways and what seems like a workable approach for me may not work for you. The key to using this book is to:-

Skim read to get a flavour of what it is about.

Reflect on each of the chapters and think about where you would like to start. You might want to dive in and write some stories or you may want to do some journaling and writing exercises.

Reread several times, as each time you read a book you will discover something new.

It is full of advice for you to try, you will get the best out of Writing to Heal by undertaking some, or all of the advice and creating ways of working that help you to use journaling and writing to help you to change your life.

JOURNAL, STORIES, OR A BOOK?

Writing to Heal is designed to inspire you to journal, and from your journal to take the next step of writing creative life stories and open you up to the possibilities of writing a book for you or for publication.

HOW DO YOU LIKE TO WORK?

The book is designed for you to dip into the parts that you need when you need them.

Please take some time out to understand yourself and how you like to work, trying to shoehorn you into my way of thinking may not work for you, but you do need to notice how you get things done and work at flexing your style.

Work in a way that suits you and which ensures that you reach your outcomes in the best way for you.

ABOUT YOU AS THE JOURNALER AND WRITER

When working with clients my job is to get the best out of them, I have to understand their learning and thinking styles, so that I can plan individual strategies to ensure that they use their journaling and writing in the most effective way.

Have you ever stopped to consider how you like to learn, what steps you take in getting things done, and why you work the way that you do? In order to be more productive and effective, we need to understand ourselves and the habits or patterns we have formed.

Aspects of journaling and writing will be easier for some than others, because each of us have preferences for the way in which we think, learn, and do. Our ways of thinking feel a 'natural' part of us and you may be unaware of these unconscious patterns until you learn to recognise them. You can learn to recognise them through your writing, language and behaviour.

Having a preference for a particular pattern can be very beneficial when that pattern is useful in a particular context. On the other hand you might find it difficult to adapt your behaviour, even when that way of doing something could be more beneficial. Consider how being more flexible with your thinking and behaviour may lead to more productive outcomes.

This section is not designed as a psychological tool, but more as a reflection of the way in which I have observed myself and my clients working, and as a review of different thinking and learning style literature. You may recognise bits out of each area or you may highly identify with one.

This is a simple guide. By understanding you, chances are you will be better equipped to get what's in your head out, onto paper and through to final publication, if publication is one of your outcomes.

If you are really interested in how you think and behave then I would highly recommend that you find someone skilled in psychometrics to help you to understand you better.

Ask yourself a few questions: -

When you go on a journey do you: -

Ask a friend for directions?

Plan the route?

Use a printed map and/or your satnav?

Just head in the general direction, you know that you will get there?

When you are have something new, do you: -

Read the instructions first?

Head to YouTube to watch how someone else does it?

Ask for help?

Just have a go (you are the ones with the left over screws)?

When you learn something new, do you: -

Watch and learn, before you do?

Talk it through with someone first?

Read it through, think about it for while, and then have a go?

Just jump in and try?

We are all different and there are reasons why some bits are easier than others. The point is, learn why you do what you do, try to flex your style or adapt the way you do things, and ask for help.

A – WHAT PEOPLE

You

Your motivation comes from inside you.

Logical, factual and results driven.

Need to research and analyse the facts.

Not easily distracted and you find it easy to focus on an activity for a set period of time.

Good time managers.

Environment

You like to work alone and in the quiet, without clutter or distractions.

Planning

You like to gather all of the information together before starting.

You like clear guidelines and facts so that you can decide what tasks need to be done and by when.

You can set achievable goals and are realistic about what needs to happen to get them done.

You test out how many words you can write an hour or day and plan accordingly.

You think through the pros and cons of how your journaling and writing methods will work.

Writing style

You are good at summarising and are concise and to the point.

You apply your logic; critically evaluate what you are writing, and use facts to support your theories.

You tend to write more about what than why, how or what if.

B – HOW PEOPLE

You

Very practical and hands on.

Want details before acting or making decisions.

You are usually on time with your projects and plans.

Environment

Neat, orderly and have a preference for quiet.

Planning

Disciplined, detailed, methodical, you like to know that there are proven methods.

Highly organised, structured, and likes a step-by-step approach, with checklists and to-do lists.

Like to try things in order to understand how you can get your plans achieved.

You like planning and having a timetable to work to.

Writing style

Very detailed, factual and clear. You would be good at writing how-to manuals or steps to change.

Tend to write more about how than why, what or what if.

C – WHY PEOPLE

You

Outgoing, sociable, emotional, and feeling, you love to work with others.

Your values are important and you like to do things based on how you feel.

You tend to need to check with others before doing things.

Great at sharing ideas.

Environment

You want to be with other people and don't mind noise or music when you are writing.

Planning

Starts enthusiastically and works intuitively and may not finish as you are easily distracted.

Has loads of ideas and trouble picking 'the' one.

Writing style

You are very creative, expressive and use emotional language.

Likes your stories to connect emotionally to your reader.

Uses creative and emotional language.

Tend to write more about who and why, than how, what or what if.

D WHAT-IF PEOPLE

You

Very curious about all sorts of things, which can lead to being easily bored and distracted. Your insights send you off in different directions.

You want the big picture, are visual, and hate details.

Keep questioning what you are working on all the time.

Need constant change, variety, and want to find different ways to do things.

Want to do it your way.

Visualise the facts, that is, you need to see things before you can make sense of them.

Environment

You like an informal, casual and fun place to work, surrounded by lovely things.

Planning

Hate to be held to a timetable and have a tendency to be unstructured.

Mind mapping works for you, as you need to see pictures of how it will work.

You must have options for different ways to tackle projects.

Writing style

You are creative and use colour, diagrams, and visuals to get your point across.

Often forget the details and find it hard to get past the big picture, conceptual, visionary stuff.

Tend to write more about what if, than how, why, or what.

THE RULES FOR EVERYONE...

Get your working environment **right for you**.

Understand your preferred way of working and behaviours.

Understand your capabilities (what skills, abilities and competencies you need to do the task).

Get your head around what you believe to be the right way and find the right way for you. Ask 'what is important to you?'

Understanding you, will help you to find a way that works for you.

Keep coming back to the purpose of your journal, stories or potential memoir or as your guide.

Don't be too hard on yourself.

Jacqui Malpass

STUFF THAT GETS IN THE WAY

"It is necessary to write, if the days are not to slip emptily by. How else, indeed, to clap the net over the butterfly of the moment? For the moment passes, it is forgotten; the mood is gone; life itself is gone." Vita Sackville-West

What things 'get in the way' of life and writing?

'Stuff' always gets in the way of everything. Doesn't it! In this section we examine what some of that might be and ways to overcome your blocks.

Welcome to journaling and creative life writing, this is going to be an adventure in finding out who you are, making great changes to your life and awakening your creative writing.

You see, once you record your behaviour, feelings and thoughts, you can then work out why you do or did what you did. You are in a fantastic position to realise your strengths, increase your potential, and get greater understanding about yourself and others.

This chapter isn't about writers block, it is about things that get in the way of getting your journaling and writing started.

The question 'does writers block exist?' leaves people in one of two camps.

If you don't believe that it exists then you will be in the camp that says when you feel resistance, just knuckle down, and get on with it.

Others say that it does exist, and that trying to keep at something when it is not working simply makes matters worse.

Whichever camp you are in, you are right.

I know as a journaler and writer there is nothing worse than looking at a blank piece of paper and not knowing what to write. Like me you will just have to face it that at some point in your writing career you will not want to write or will let things get in the way.

I find my inspiration often comes at the oddest moments and not when I am poised, fingers ready, at my computer.

However, whatever your perception, there are, in my view, things that get in the way. Some of what gets in the way is as a result of choices you make and some as a result of things out of your control.

You have to identify what is getting in the way and then take action to end your inaction. We are talking psychology here, and not our inability to string a few words together.

Journaling and writing, we know, needs discipline and commitment. First step for me every time is to remind myself of values, passions, purpose, and vision. That's in the chapter called Getting from Values to Vision.

Take time to understand what motivates you to write and talk to a coach or a friend if you are unsure and need some clarity.

Let's look at perceived common blocks to journaling and writing and look at ways to get past them.

FEAR, UNCERTAINTY AND DOUBT – FUD

FUD is generally a strategic attempt to influence perception by disseminating negative and dubious or false information.

Gene Amdahl originally defined FUD (Fear, Uncertainty, and Doubt) after he left IBM to found his own company. He used it to describe the fear, uncertainty, and doubt that the IBM sales people were spreading to their customers who might be considering the competition's products. In this case the competition was Amdahl.

In terms of your journaling and writing, it is your perception that is spreading the FUD and leaving you unable to move forward.

Perception

Perception is everything. What comes in through our senses is processed through our filters and becomes our truth. This is imprinted in our minds and so it is.

In reverse what we think also becomes our truth.

Just consider that for a moment. What we think becomes our truth. Writing and gaining aha moments allows us to change our perception. When it is in black and white, staring you in the face, your pen now has the power to help you to change your perception.

Remember, it's always your choice.

What kinds of fud are there?

There are different kinds of FUD that I come across:-

I am scared someone will find my journals and writing.

I am too busy.

I can't think of what to write next.

There is no time.

What I have written is boring.

I don't know what to write about.

I don't know where to start.

I can't write stories.

I am scared of failing (or is that success?).

My creativity upped and went!

Who will want to read what I have to say?

There are already lots of books on my subject.

Writing to Heal

I want to journal and write but.... (You fill in the blanks)

What I propose is this. At many times of our lives FUD will appear. It will appear as the voices in our heads, AKA the mind chatter, that endless, relentless stream of thoughts that wanders around our minds distracting and demotivating us. When your mind is full of rubbish it is hard to concentrate on other things.

This is when writing really is your best friend. When I say writing, I mean journaling. Leave what you are doing and get scribbling, it doesn't matter if it seems incoherent or meaningless, get it down and then let it rest awhile. When you come back to whatever it was you were writing about, you will have much more clarity.

Harness your FUD and turn it into something creative and useful. Having these feelings is usually a sign that you are onto something good, but the voices want to tell you otherwise. We have choices and it is your choice if you or the voices win.

Fear

I also want to challenge you and ask if you have a crystal ball? Can you see into the future and know, absolutely know that you will fail or that everyone will think your work is rubbish? Fear can be translated into

False evidence appearing real.

Fear is an unpleasant emotion or thought. It is the feeling you get when you are afraid or worried that something bad is going to happen. Fear can be real or imaginary, and you experience it because of your misperception or misjudgement of a situation. It causes you to feel anxiety, insecurity, and a complete lack of positive feeling.

Fear is also necessary for survival.

Fear is usually about some unknown future event that may never happen. When we sense danger – real or imagined – our body reacts because our primary drive is to survive, we feel unsafe, so we simply don't write or take any other action. Use your perceived fear as a survival tool in the jungle of life.

Uncertainty

The only certainty is uncertainty, just as the only thing we know about change is that it will continue to happen. As with fear, we simply do not and cannot know the future outcome, with one exception; we know for certain (or do we) that one day we will die.

I'd like to think that by the time that certainty appears, you and I will have made our mark on the world with our words.

Just like the film Uncertainty, where on the flip of a coin, our young couple could have a day at her parents or something else more frightening and sinister could happen.

Will you flip a coin and take a chance or will you harness your uncertainty creativity, construct some well-formed outcomes(Chapter – Values to Vision), and put actions into place? Whatever gets in the way now will be down to your choices.

And if you really want to confuse yourself Google the uncertainty principle about how to calculate certainty.

Doubt

Doubt is about being stuck between belief and non-belief and may also be linked to lack of faith. We all have experienced anger and frustration about our perceived ability to write, it is normal.

Look at your thesaurus for some of the words that are offered as alternative negative words. Hesitation, uncertainty, reservation, misgiving, distrust, disbelief, qualm, suspicion, scepticism, have reservations, faithlessness, lack of confidence.

Then consider the opposite. Belief, certainty, confidence, dependence, faith, reliance, and trust.

PROCRASTINATION

FUD leads to procrastination which is linked to our beliefs and therefore we must understand what those beliefs are and how we can overcome them. Common beliefs like:-

Perfection - everything must be perfect before I start my journal.

Being certain - you need to ensure that you know everything before you start.

I need help - instead of starting you always think that you need somebody else to help you.

Failure / success - you fear either success or failure.

This is the right way - when you are told that this is the way to do it, you simply rebel and don't start because you can.

Your environment - you don't start because you think your environment is not right.

You want it easy - you believe journaling and writing is easy and forget that it requires motivation and dedication.

What we need to do is find out what your procrastination beliefs are and find a way to overcome them.

Leap of faith to end FUD and procrastination

Let's take a leap of faith, be brave, and turn our thoughts, ideas, and words into art to share. One way of overcoming this is to have a **Procrastination Action Plan** – as a way of responding to the excuses you come up with.

Your Procrastination Action Plan is a list of the things you procrastinate over and next to each your solution. What happens when you decide what the solutions are, you get some of the wonderful light bulb moments and you know exactly what you have to do.

Another way is to consider ways to break the FUD cycle.

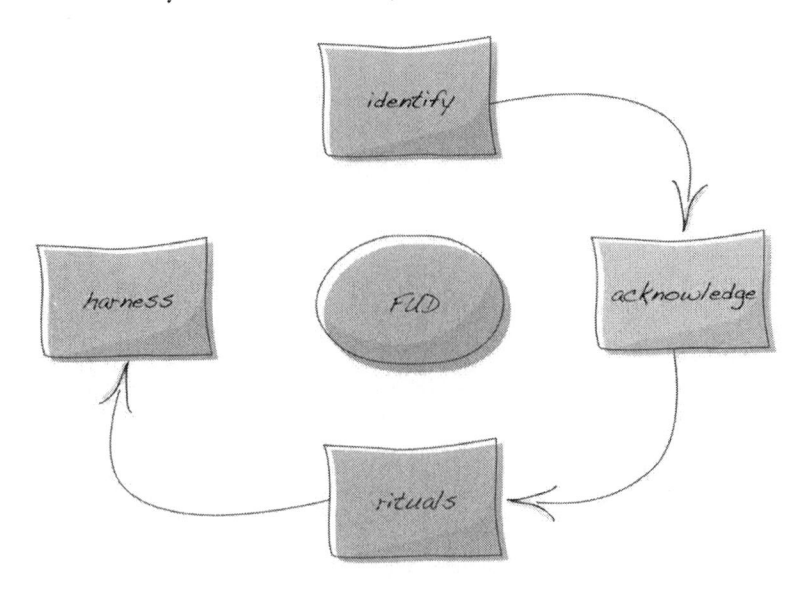

1. Identify your thoughts, when you have them, what can you see, feel, and hear?
2. Acknowledge them...
3. Create rituals to overcome them.
4. Harness the energy of rituals and creatively use them to create a better state for writing.

Rituals

Before you start to write, create a ritual. This might be:-

Bath.

Meditation.

Cup of tea and raw chocolate treat.

Light a candle.

Put eucalyptus (or an uplifting oil that you like) in an oil burner.

Set the clock for a 30 minute journaling and writing session.

Write.

The main point is that you recognise the emotions which come up for you and you create a process that helps you before, during, and after. What rituals would work for you?

Going into meltdown

There will be times when your journaling or writing causes you so much pain that you get into a cycle of not wanting to write, because you know what will happen.

Really? You really know? Or do you think you know and by telling yourself that you know, you do.

The pain that you are feeling is meant to be. No matter how painful this is, it really is about releasing and letting go, and here's the thing - you have a **choice** about what you do about it and what you do next.

PRIVACY

Although I adore the feel of the pen on paper, and the way that unconscious thoughts simply flow, my prime instinct is to have my raw thoughts and feelings locked away where only I can read them.

Use a computer package with encrypted software.

Find a good hiding place.

Decide 'who cares?' If someone snoops and finds something they don't like, then tough, they shouldn't have looked.

Ask others to respect your privacy.

Lock it in a safe place.

HONESTY

Having a journal is an opportunity to be honest with yourself and it can sometimes be difficult to let go and say it as it is. We can learn a lot from our honesty, and when we write from a place which is full of emotion it is far better than any skilled writer could ever achieve.

When it comes from your gut and not your head you will learn so much about yourself. Let your values shine through your writing.

Accept that your unconscious mind wants you to know whatever it is telling you.

Reflect on what you have written, what does it really tell you?

Face the truth and take action.

PERMISSION

Permission to be you. When you write in a private journal and know that your thoughts are safe, that there aren't any reasons not to write, you can give yourself permission to write from the heart.

Once you feel comfortable with journaling and writing and have given yourself permission there will be nothing to stand in the way of you and your truth. It doesn't matter that you haven't recorded the last 20, 30, 40 years, today is the perfect day to start your story.

Do you really need permission to write? Identify what is worrying you and then take action. Accept it and move on.

TELLING TALES

Keeping a journal is not about telling tales or made up stories, it is about being blunt and truthful, whilst maintaining your personal integrity. Write as it is.

It is really important that you just write naturally, it doesn't matter if you can't spell or if your grammar leaves a lot to be desired, this is not a writing competition; this is your journal and your life.

The rule is, there are no rules.

This journal is yours, the way you write in it, how you use it, is yours and yours alone. Nobody can tell you what to do or how to do it.

HANDWRITING

It really doesn't matter about the state of your handwriting, what is wonderful when you keep a written journal of any form is it you will start to notice changes in the way that you write and these will be reflected by the kind of mood you're in. This is also a great barometer for you. And it doesn't matter if anybody else can read your writing as long as you can.

The fact that no-one can read your writing is brilliant.

Use a computer if it really bothers you.

Our writing is a reflection of our minds. Analyse it and have some fun reading into your moods.

HOW TO CHANGE HABITS AND PATTERNS OF BEHAVIOUR

As children we learn from the adults around us. We study hard and learn how to perfect the art of the adult. As this happens through our childlike perceptions of the world we learn patterns, habits, and beliefs. We become containers for others' energy and these imprint on our minds and souls.

In attempting to understand the ways of the world and our fellow humans, we innocently process and analyse information and create our own perceptions. The more we see something acted out, the more it reinforces our belief that it is true.

And so the habits of our life form. What we do today is probably much the same as yesterday and will be for many days to come. Whatever those habits are they make us who we are.

The key to great habits and unwinding the not so good ones is awareness and knowing that they don't serve us and that by taking small steps you can change them, one habit at a time.

If you took just one habit, made some alterations and did that for 30 or more days, you would, I guarantee, make changes. I put a rider on this, because one of the things we tend to do when we have succeeded at overcoming a challenge is congratulating ourselves and self-sabotaging.

The key is to do something different.

Changing habits

There are many techniques you can consider such as:-

Use a trigger – if you struggle with journaling and writing and want to form a habit of giving yourself just 30 minutes, set an alarm to tell you it's writing time and then set another alarm when there are just 10 minutes left.

Replace needs – if you decide to give up TV, what could you do instead? You might listen to the radio or music. But if you didn't have something to fill the gap, you would soon be switching the TV back on. Fill that time with writing.

Make it a pleasure – if making changes is painful then clearly something is wrong. If going to the gym is something you hate, why go? Remember to be patient and kind to yourself, if you fall off the horse, get back on, adjust your seat, and carry on.

But and And – when you feel yourself saying something negative, write it out and follow the negartive with a 'but' or an 'and' and writing something positive. E.g. *It was a horrible day, but in retrospect, it meant that I could... (something positive).*

Write – well of course as you would expect that from a book on Journaling and writing, Write, it is cathartic and proven to work therapeutically to enable change.

Accountability – If getting started is difficult, ask a friend to hold you accountable and ring you at an agreed time for you to start your journal or writing, or to ask you what you are writing about this week. Make an agreement that they can 'not take any shit from you.' If you have someone to hold you accountable, chances are you will stick to it. And if you feel brave enough you could share your writing and get feedback.

KISS – keep it simple (silly), why make change hard.

Keep at it – same time, every day. My journaling is a night time in bed habit, my blogging and other writing is an early morning habit. It works for me, try it.

Try difference – play around until you find ways a new habit will work for you. Just because it works for me, doesn't mean that it will work for you. We are all different.

Limiting self-beliefs

When your inner critic pops up her ugly head, keep a note of what she is saying. Come back to your critic after a walk, sleep, cup of tea and write, giving her some advice.

Fear

One way to learn to face your fears is to write them down and then create some kind of dialogue around them, or look at them from another's perspective.

Another way to overcome fear is to recognise when you feel the fear trigger, make a note of what happened in the lead up, your emotions, what you saw, felt or heard, then ask yourself:-

What is the worst thing that could happen?

What is the best thing that could happen?

Introduce your own self-talk series so that when you notice you are getting fearful for no apparent reason, switch to positive self-talk.

Expectations of perfection

Think about this - if it is never written, you will never know just how good, compelling, interesting or life changing it is. Will you?

Everyone is good at something. Journaling and writing, like anything, takes time to shape. Be a happy writer, because you can enjoy the process of journaling and writing. What you are writing about will change your life and very possibly someone else's. Make the choice to break from perfection, start being creative and stop being perfect.

Going around in circles

Being perfect kills creativity – stop, write just one word, leave it, and fill in the rest later. Use that word as the basis for some research.

Permission

Do you really need permission to journal or write? Identify what is worrying you and then take action. Perhaps talk it through with someone else.

Distraction

Prepare for distraction, by that I mean get your journaling and writing space and environment ready.

Turn off your distractions – Facebook, Twitter and phone.

Set a timer, you can go off and play later.

Wear headphones and listen to music.

Put a sign up – Go away and leave me alone…

Make your own distraction busting list and do them.

Buy some Freedom. - Pay around $10 for a programme called Freedom (http://macfreedom.com) which will turn off all of your distractions for a set period of time.

Mind chatter

Prepare for mind chatter – pick a song or do your 5 times table in your head when it starts.

Put the tip of your tongue on the roof of your mouth.

Doodle.

Go and do something else – Facebook, Twitter and phone (yes, really).

Do something else

When you are faced with overwhelm or lack of motivation, stop and find another activity.

Make lists of things you want to write about, take one, and just write.

Go for a walk, take a Dictaphone with you, and talk about what is on your mind.

Take time out to reflect.

Write on multiple subjects. I quite like this as I like the freshness of writing about something new.

Change your space. I write in my office, sun house, bed, on the sofa, with music, with silence. Whatever it takes to make me feel comfortable at that time.

Brainstorm ideas for what comes next. Leave them to marinate and let your unconscious decide what comes next.

Do some research on your subject and see what others are saying, this will usually spark something in your imagination.

QUESTIONS TO ASK YOURSELF WHEN FACED WITH A CHALLENGE.

What's the problem?

How long have you had the problem?

Why do you have this problem?

Who is to blame for you having this problem?

Why haven't you solved it yet?

What do you want?

How will you know when you've got what you want?

What resources do you already have that will enable you to solve this problem?

When have you succeeded in solving a similar problem before?

What is the next step?

10 questions is courtesy of Dr Bridget Kirsop

What do you perceive as standing in your way?

What is your plan to overcome your FUD and procrastination?

Jacqui Malpass

WRITING FROM THE HEART

"Writing became such a process of discovery that I couldn't wait to get to work in the morning: I wanted to know what I was going to say." Sharon O'Brien

Why does writing from the heart make a difference?

STEPPING STONE

Love, just a step away

If you want me, I am here

Throw off your worries, shed your past

Step beside me, feel the blast

I hold your heart, it caresses my soul

A lifetime of journeys yet untold

We touch across time, together again

Your memory carries me onwards

I look in your eyes and see my soul

Heart to heart on stepping stones

WRITING FROM THE HEART

It is vital that we journal and write from the right place, in the right frame of mind, that we let go of our self-consciousness, become one with ourselves and write without judgment. If you write from your head, your left logical brain is engaged, in writing from your heart you will open up the space for you to love and to be loved. When we take responsibility for loving ourselves then our lives can change.

Hearts get broken and unbalanced by our relationships with ourselves and others. By writing from your heart you can let go and start walking towards the person you know that you are.

Healing has to come from within you. Our writing can take us to the depths of despair or the soaring heights of ecstasy. Neither place is balanced.

There is too much noise going on around us, too many people want our time, money, a part of us, and we hand it over readily. We become a part of the overall sound rather than one unique note, which is us.

By looking inwards we will find our words, the bits of our writing, which will make the melodies of our lives.

When I write from deep within myself I am shocked and amazed at what I write, it is if someone else has penned the words, yet they resonate, bring clarity and meaning to my life.

By bringing your pain to the forefront of your being, experiencing it, you will be able to find your own resources to carry you forward.

Just write with all of your heart and soul let the story flow and in letting go, release your pain.

Don't waste your pain - use it.

Take your focus to your heart. Put your pen to paper and just start writing, write quickly. After 5 minutes, stop. What emotions does this writing evokes in you?

It is important that the emotions are spontaneous and not written with lots of thought. In this way you can lay bare and expose what your heart wants you to know and to deal with. What does your world look like from your heart?

Allow the real you to shine.

When you have connected your heart to your pen, you will find that you are writing about what you care about and when you care, it will flow.

What is your relationship with you?

What does your heart tell you it wants to write about?

Whose heart do you want to connect to?

Writing to Heal

IN THE WRITERS RUCKSACK

"Much as I like owning a Rolls-Royce, I could do without it. What I could not do without is a typewriter, a supply of yellow second sheets and the time to put them to good use."
John O'Hara

What tools do I need in my writers rucksack?

Every good journaler and writer needs their rucksack stuffed with relevant things for their journey; they make the job of writing easier. What should go in yours?

WHAT SHOULD PACK FOR YOUR JOURNEY?

Having the right tools and resources makes it easier to get started and stay on track. Your writers' rucksack contains a set of useful ways of working, gadgets, and devices that will enable you to make your writing life easier. This chapter provides you with a list of the tools you might like to pack.

Journal

Journaling is, in my opinion, the foundation of all writing. Think of it as a place to store your raw materials, your ideas, thoughts, processes, reflections on your book and random musings.

Journal each day (if you can), write quickly and freely, don't think, just write. I call this freestyle writing. Sitting in silence, with either your eyes open or closed, let the images, feelings, and sounds of the day, wander into your mind. Just let them come to you, and notice what you notice. Let your unconscious mind work.

Keep it all, even if it seems disjointed and doesn't flow, even if you feel embarrassed when you read it back. Keep it; it will be useful and insightful.

Notebook

Keep a little notebook in your bag/briefcase or upon your person somewhere, as you go about your day-to-day activities and as you spot something, just make a few notes, you can refer back to your notebook when you come to write in your journal.

Computer and printer

I am a techno geek, I love technology as an enabler, and I want software and systems which makes my life easier. Make a list of what you need and get yourself the best equipment that your budget allows. A desktop computer is great, but how will you take that to different locations to write? For me a notebook computer is a must every time.

Video or voice recording

With the advent of digital cameras and digital camcorders there are lots of opportunity to be able capture 'those moments' to video. This adds an extra dimension to your journaling and writing.

Video, along with a Dictaphone or the recorder on your mobile phone, is a great way to collect random thoughts and ideas. In each listening you learn something new.

Voice translation

Dragon NaturallySpeaking or Dragon Dictate on a Mac allows you to talk to your computer. Dragon will interpret what you say and type as you speak. I love this software, though be aware it may record some odd words.

You can talk faster than you can type and for the dedicated talker you could get over 20,000 words done in a weekend. Which is great for those of you who do want to take your stories and turn them into a book.

Making backups

There is nothing more frustrating than losing your work. Backup, backup, backup. You can back up to places like Dropbox (www.dropbox.com) and Google Drive, a USB stick and to an external hard drive. The key is to do this on a regular basis. I save everything to Dropbox and then copy my writing folder to Google Drive, then make a copy for my computer and, once a month, back everything up to an external hard drive.

WHO SHOULD YOU TAKE ALONG FOR THE JOURNEY?

Get a coach

It's easy to give up. When we are alone, we listen to our negative thoughts more than our positive thoughts. It's not always easy to be our own coach. A good coach will keep you motivated and moving.

When you are stuck or resistant, fed up, procrastinating, your coach is by your side or at the end of the phone or email. He or she has the experience and knowledge to know what needs to be done to help you to reach your outcomes. They will hold you accountable, keep you on track, challenge you, have fun with you, share resources and a whole host of other things and you would be mad to pay for someone's time and not maximise it.

If your journaling, stories, or memoir raises personal issues and upsets, discuss this with your coach who may be suitably trained to help you. If not, they can advise where to go to get professional help for the area that you are struggling with.

What needs to go into your rucksack to make your journey easier?

Who can help carry your bags?

Let's start now

Open your journal and write the following…

Today's date. Today is the first day of my journal. I have made a promise to myself and that is I am going to write in my journal regularly.

There you go, you have started! What else can you write?

Jacqui Malpass

STARTING TO JOURNAL AND WRITE

"Words are, of course, the most powerful drug used by mankind." Rudyard Kipling

How do I start to write and journal?

You would think that writing in a journal would be really easy. For some that is just not the case. In this section, I offer some hints and tips which will help you to start and keep going, plus some ideas which will help you journal and write.

GETTING INTO A GREAT STATE

The first thing that I do is to get into the right frame of mind to start writing in my journal; this includes dealing with all the mundane tasks that need doing. I make sure I'm in loose clothing (often my pyjamas as I love to write in bed), I have a cup of tea, that my partner knows it's time for me to write and I am in a warm comfortable place. If my jaw is clenched or I feel tense in some way, I take a few moments to focus on my breathing.

TAKING A PERSONAL INVENTORY

It is a good idea before you start to write that you take a personal inventory. Do not change anything, just notice what you notice.

Body awareness

Sit quietly for a few moments and become aware of your body, take your attention to your toes, now let your awareness move up your body through every single part. Feel which parts feel uncomfortable and which parts feel comfortable.

Breathe into each uncomfortable part and let it go. You could imagine that it is a piece of newspaper, which is old news. Scrunch it up and throw it away.

Mental pictures

What mental pictures do you have at the moment? Where are they? How far away are they from you? Are they in colour or in black-and-white?

The sounds around you

As you sit quietly what sounds do you notice? Are there sounds in the room? Can you hear sounds in the distance? Are you talking to yourself? What sort of things are you saying to yourself?

BALANCING

You need to stand up to this one, place your feet hip distance apart, let your hands hang by your sides, close your eyes and feel a sense of where you are in the room. Are you leaning to one side? Are you falling forwards or backwards? What needs to happen to rebalance you? Get a sense of balance and then open your eyes.

STATE OF MIND

This is a great exercise to do when you're feeling a little bit disoriented or maybe when you're about to start reflecting, it is a great starting point.

Sitting down, close your eyes.

Ask yourself what is your current state of mind.

Ask yourself what is your most dominant emotion.

Come back to the present.

If your most dominant emotion is negative, what has to happen to turn that into a positive one? If it is positive, what can you do to hold on to it and really enjoy it?

GRATITUDE

When you are feeling rubbish and think that the world is against you take a tip from Rhonda Byrne and write 10 things you are grateful for, right at this moment. Once you start it is really quite liberating and illuminating. You could just be grateful for your cup of tea.

MEDITATION

Meditation is the practice of entering a higher state of consciousness that brings about a sense and a state of calm, which has been reported to enhance psychological balance and emotional stability.

The goal of meditation is the elimination or reduction or slowing of your internal dialogue. The aim is to take your attention away from the day to day stuff and be able to observe it from a detached state.

For some journalers and writers having a meditation prior to writing and reflection enhances the experience.

Chakra meditation

Find a comfortable place to sit or lie. Close your eyes. Take some deep breaths.

Become aware of your body from head to toe, of your weight, of the heaviness of your limbs.

Imagine a shaft of light extending from the base of your spine into the earth and travelling into the centre of the earth. Breathe in deep red light and breathe out any negative things that you may be holding inside you. Do this a few times.

Now imagine that there are roots growing from the bottom of your feet and growing into the earth. You are now securely anchored into the ground.

Next, extend the shaft from the base of your spine into the heavens and breathe in pure white light and breathe out any negative things that you may be holding inside you. Do this a few times.

You should now be feeling relaxed.

Starting with the **root chakra**, place your hands at the bottom of your hips, and focus on the area at the base of the spine, the area between your legs.

The colour of the root chakra is red. Focus on the chakra. What does it look like or feel like? Imagine a large red swirling circle over your root chakra; see if there are any dark areas, in your mind's eye clear them away until you see a clean clear red circle.

Take a few deep breaths and now move onto your sacral chakra.

Place your hands on your abdomen, to the area of the "womb."

The colour of the **sacral chakra** is orange. Focus on the chakra. What does it look like or feel like. Imagine a large orange swirling circle over your sacral chakra, see if there are any dark areas, in your mind's eye clear them away until you see a clean clear orange circle.

Take a few deep breaths and move your hands up to your **solar plexus chakra**.

Place your hands on your stomach.

The colour of the solar plexus chakra is yellow. Focus on the chakra. What does it look like or feel like? Imagine a large yellow swirling circle over your solar plexus chakra, see if there are any dark areas, in your mind's eye clear them away until you see a clean clear yellow circle.

Take a few deep breaths.

Now turn your attention to the middle of your chest, to the **heart chakra**, the green (or pink) chakra. Place your hands here. Take a few deep breaths.

The colour of the heart chakra is green or pink. Focus on the chakra. What does it look like or feel like? Imagine a large green or pink swirling circle over your heart chakra, see if there are any dark areas, in your mind's eye clear them away until you see clean clear green or pink circle.

Take a few deep breaths.

Now focus on the throat, place your hands here. Take a few deep breaths.

The colour of the **throat chakra** is blue. Focus on the chakra. What does it look like or feel like? Imagine a large blue swirling circle over your throat chakra, see if there are any dark areas, in your mind's eye clear them away until you see a clean clear blue circle.

Take a few deep breaths.

Now focus on the middle of your forehead, the third eye. Place your hands here. Take a few deep breaths.

The colour of the **third eye chakra** is indigo. Focus on the chakra. What does it look like or feel like? Imagine a large indigo swirling circle over your third eye chakra, see if there are any dark areas, in your mind's eye clear them away until you see a clean clear indigo circle.

Take a few deep breaths.

Now focus your attention at the crown of your head. Place your hands here and take a few deep breaths.

The colour of the **crown chakra** is violet. Focus on the chakra. What does it look like or feel like? Imagine a large violet swirling circle over your crown chakra, see if there are any dark areas, in your mind's eye, and clear them away until you see a clean clear violet circle.

Take a few deep breaths.

All your chakras are now clean, charged and in balance.

Now mentally go back down through your chakras and imagine a flower closing and close each one.

Take a few deep breaths, choose a colour that you like, and breathe it out all around you, and imagine you are cocooned in beautiful light.

When you feel ready open your eyes.

You are completely refreshed, calm, and peaceful.

Your energy is balanced. You are full of vitality.

Pick up your pen and start to write

MAKING A DATE

Dating your entries is really useful and a great habit to get into. You will start to see cycles and patterns in the things that are happening in your life; you will also be able to file things away in some chronological order and of course, by dating things, you will be able to see where the gaps in your journaling and writing are. Ask, why didn't you journal or write on those days?

THE DAILY JOURNAL

There are two ways that people mainly like to journal, one is freestyle where they let the unconscious unravel, and the second way is to use structure where you use questions as prompts.

When you start your journal journey, it is useful to try both. In this way you will know what works best for you. Like me, you may find that both are useful depending upon your mood.

The daily Journal is about your relationship with your life. Your daily entry is what keeps you up-to-date with what is happening, and is where you come back to reflect.

Freestyle

Freestyle is writing as if no one will ever read it. A bit like dance like no one is watching – just let go.

To describe how to do it is difficult. I 'put my mind' somewhere else, sort of like switching off, put my pen on the paper, and just write. I suppose this is kind of trance like.

When I am writing short stories or yet another chapter of my 'one day I will publish a novel' book, I read back through the story so far and ask myself where do I want to take this today, whilst focusing inwards. Then I start to write and just continue the story.

When I write a blog, I think of the title and what I imagine would be useful for anyone to know, write it and then ask myself, well, what do you think, how would you solve that and then write the answers that come up.

We each have our own way of doing this. Find it, love it, and just do it.

Questions - structure

Of course, things are so much easier if someone asks us questions. So here goes. Try these.

How did the day begin?

What happened as the day progressed?

What is today's story?

What is the best thing that happened?

What am I grateful for today?

How did the day end?

You must journal and write in the way that suits your style. If you were drawn to one style more than another, please have a go at writing another style, notice how it feels and what you can learn from it.

The most important thing when you write freestyle or structured is that you write quickly and spontaneously. This will engage the creative right side of your brain and of course, when you do something quickly and without thinking you are using your unconscious mind.

The only time that we want to use the conscious part of our brain is when we come back to reflect and even then, intuition is just as important.

Here's what I do

I use both freestyle and structured. I enjoy traveling inside myself, putting my pen to paper and allowing a stream of unconscious thoughts to come forth. I am often amazed at what I write when I use this style. I do this best when I use a pen and paper.

By the side of my bed is my journal and pen, I use it to scribble my thoughts, doodles, short stories, blog and other ideas in. Just before going to sleep is a great time for me to do this, as I get the things out that need to be settled before sleeping.

Other ways I journal is to use software like Journal 5 which is secure and allows me to create a structure to my journal writing. I like the structure and privacy which it gives me, enabling me to be totally and utterly honest in what I write. Within this system I'm able to keep different sections for different things, for example:-

My daily Journal.

People log.

Eating, exercise and body talk.

Random memories.

My now - where I find myself right now.

Personal feedback and reflection.

I journal sporadically, sometimes daily and sometimes every few days. I do what suits me. I like both structure and freeform creativity, not at the same time of course, so when the mood takes me I do what is right for me at that time.

To help me, when I can't write, I simply do something else, such as walk my dog, and I often take a Dictaphone to record my thoughts. I look silly walking around talking to myself; however I can record lots of information. When I get home I translate this by listening back and typing or by using some software called Dragon Naturally Speaking, which I dictate into and it then types it up for me. What I am trying to say is that there are many ways to journal and write, just find what suits you, and do it.

FINDING YOUR STYLE

Be authentic, be yourself, use your intuition, and develop your style and the things you want to journal and write about. Of course, you can go to class to learn about the craft of writing and pick up some great creative writing tips. At the end of the day, journaling and writing is what you want it to be.

LOOKING FOR INSPIRATION
Doodling

When you can't find the words, doodle. Doodling essentially allows our intuitive feelings to come out in pictures and symbols.

Interpreting these pictures and symbols can help to reveal meanings that are not apparent to our linear mind. A picture or symbol conveys an entire thought in one image. While doodling, words may form themselves, and these should be accepted. But, for the most part, doodling allows the unconscious to come to the surface without judgment or critical analysis from the conscious mind. Therefore, if you find yourself doodling, that's great, carry on.

Mind Mapping

When I am stuck for putting structure around something I simply create a mind map.

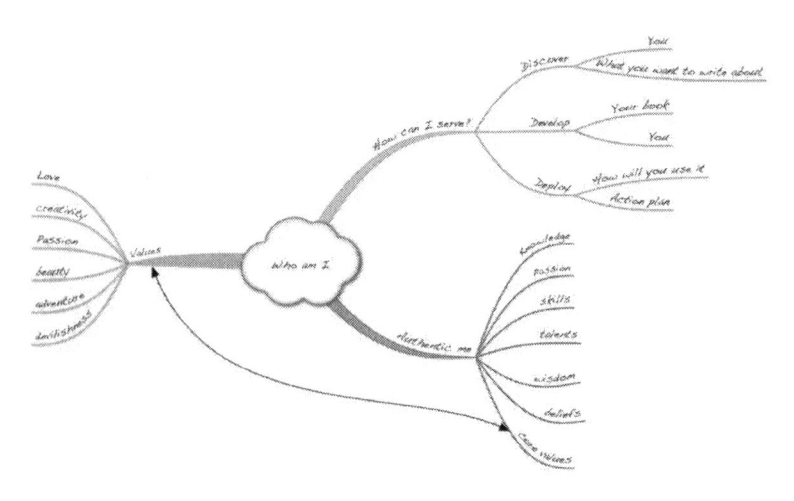

A mind map is a collection of thoughts around a central idea. It is quick and simple and serves to ignite my imagination. I also use it for creating plans and developing ideas.

Kick-starts

Kick-starts are any inspiration which kick-starts your journaling and writing. Often it is something that just triggers your imagination or a stirring of a memory.

For example, someone you are talking to, mentions the Grand Canyon and you are back on your holiday, winding your way through the red rocks.

There are lots of books or online articles which can provide kick-starts, go with your intuition and pick something and just write. This book contains lots of ideas for kick-starts.

Feel good list

Your feel good list is basically a to-do list with a difference as it contains things that truly affect your life. They will be areas you want to explore more deeply, the ones that will make a difference to your life!

What's most important to you?

What deserves more of your time?

What do you want to be or do in your lifetime?

What, when you think about it really makes you feel good?

Put your feel good list into a priority order and when you are stuck for inspiration, pick a topic, and write and reflect on what is it about that item that is really important to you.

Books, magazines proverbs and quotes,

Pick up a book or magazine, close your eyes, open the book or magazine at any random page, and point your finger. Where your finger lands, read what is there and use one of the words or sentences to start you off. Proverbs are brilliant at giving you a kick start, how about these:-

A leopard can't change its spots.

It's no use crying over spilt milk.

A woman's work is never done.

The calm before the storm.

Quotes get me every time and I always wish that I had been the person to have said them. Try these:-

In the end, it's not going to matter how many breaths you took, but how many moments took your breath away - Shing Xiong

When life gives you a hundred reasons to cry, show life that you have a thousand reasons to smile.

Be who you are and say what you feel because those who mind don't matter and those who matter don't mind. - Dr. Seuss

Explore what provokes your emotions, what do you hear, see, feel, smell, or taste, what does this item mean to you? Where do your inspiration pieces take you?

Prompts

If you could be anywhere with anyone doing whatever you wanted to do, what would it be?

What was the highlight of your day, the best moment you can remember?

Describe the most important thing in your life. Describe the 2nd and 3rd most important things. Then the 4th and 5th most important things.

What or who is the most influential thing in your life today?

Ask yourself what you would like to dream about. Pretend you are dreaming. Write in detail about the dream you are having. Try to affect what is happening and then choose to have things happen without your control.

As you go about your day, stop at quarter past each hour and make a note of what is in front of you.

Writing to Heal

Write down the opposite of what you see, hear or feel.

Make a celebration day, what would it be and how would you celebrate?

Pick a headline in the news, how would you solve the problem, what would you have done differently, how do you feel about the item?

What 3 things must you finish today?

Writing stories just for fun

Write for 15 minutes on any of the following, make your own up, or open a book and follow the first sentence that you see.

He passed me the goddess of business voodoo doll…

The old photo looked vaguely familiar, where had I seen him/her before?

I was driving along the old dual carriageway from Jerez to Gibraltar, when I saw…

The house, although wrecked, had a fancy roll top bath, sitting in the vacant bathroom…

His cowboy boots were scuffed and his jacket stained, as he handed over his fiver I noticed…

She was drooling; it made me feel…

The evening began like any other, until the phone rang. It was a call that…

BEING ORIGINAL

Your journal is the origin of your life and experiences and as such provides a wealth of unique material. Record everything; you never know where you can use it.

Think about the stories that you will write, your memoirs, or a book to help others.

WHAT WILL YOU DO WITH YOUR WRITING?

Whilst we are on the subject of your writing, what will you do with yours?

Nothing, it will be your private recording that no one will ever see.

Reflection, you will use it to reflect on your life and make changes.

Blogging, you will start an online blog and use some of it for stories and comments.

Write a book, you will want to write a book (novel, non-fiction or your memoirs) and your journal is where you keep your inspiration, characters, and plots.

What has to happen to get your journaling and writing started?

Where will you find your inspiration?

What will you do with your journaling and writing?

"I always knew looking back on the tears would make me laugh, but I never knew looking back on the laughs would make me cry." – Unknown

TIMELINES

"The real voyage of discovery consists not in seeking new landscapes, but in having new eyes." Marcel Proust

How does a timeline help me to find themes for healing?

THE JOURNEY

Cascade through time

Thoughts tumble

Reason, not rhyme

Time, too short

Life, a journey

Love

We wonder why?

Death

In essence, reborn

TIMELINES

Stuffed away in the time capsule of your mind are millions of memories. They are locked away in folders with little tags on that say 'been there, done that, no longer interesting'. It is only when you pull out the folders and scatter the papers on the floor can you see connections. Scribbled on the sepia tinted parchments of time are your stories. As you put these into categories and re-file them away in a different order a new map of your life will emerge.

Timelines provide a visual roadmap, which give you the big picture in the form of a map. Clarity will come because the human mind sees things in patterns. When you see patterns you make connections. When you connect the map of your life to your values, purpose, passion, and vision, a clearing to the pathway for your stories and possible memoir or book will emerge.

No matter where you are, discovery through timelines is a vital part of discovering connections and patterns about your life, enabling you to see where your stories are and how they connect. Discovery is about going deeper and resurfacing more about your life. Regardless of career path or life roles, you will have learnt and experienced an enormous amount and very often these are things that you take for granted.

Before you create your timeline here are a few time related exercises.

WHERE IS MY NOW?

Everyone's perception of time is different. Use this exercise to put your journaling and writing into a timeframe and into context, so that when you reflect you are able to consider more clearly how events that surround your life are affecting you and how things fit together.

Your now will have been triggered by an event, this may be an event that happened a year, a month, a week, a day, or even just an hour ago.

I find it best to get comfortable, relax and to let my mind wander as I ask each question. It may be that you need to run through the list of questions, then go and do something else and come back to reflect.

Your now questions

Ask yourself the question, where am I now in my life?

When did my now start?

What was the trigger?

What has been happening in my now?

What are the main characteristics of my now?

What images, sounds, feelings, come to mind?

Who are you having relationships with? Write down the names and what they mean to you.

What projects are you working on? Write down what they are, and how they fit into your life.

What is making you happy or sad at this time?

What frustrations or tensions are you feeling?

How is your health? Focus on your body and make a note of what you notice.

What exercise or me time are you having?

What is your diet like? Are you eating sensibly, or eating rubbish, are there any cravings?

Write quickly, briefly, and write unconsciously.

TIMELINES

Timelines are a useful way to discover locked away thoughts, memories, skills, talents, experiences. Their value comes from **observing and reflecting** on what has been captured on the paper, your visual storyboard. When you stand back and observe your life you gain a lot of clarity. You also need to be prepared to keep walking away to reflect, coming back and trying to see what is missing or what needs moving around You are looking for patterns, connections, and themes..

Start brainstorming

Get a large sheet of paper and with a set of post-it notes or coloured pens / pencils and put your date of birth at one end and today's date at another.

Next divide the paper up into decades (across the top - horizontally).

Along the side put in your themes – this will naturally depend on you and what you want to write about, e.g. Career, relationships, journeys, health.

Start brainstorming, just do it randomly. As a thought comes to mind put it down.

When you have brainstormed, reflect and start moving your thoughts around.

Look for connections, themes and aha moments.

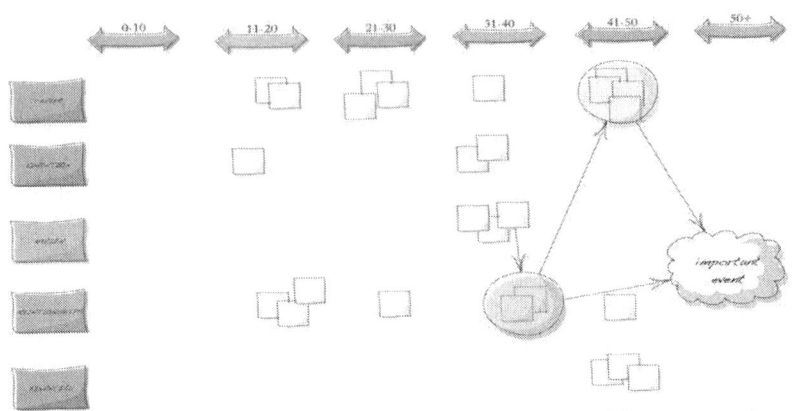

Once you can see the connections, you will be able to see where your healing themes are. For example, things that happened in childhood may have created a lack of self-worth as an adult, which in turn has meant that you have always chosen partners who are abusive. Alternatively, you have always settled for mediocre jobs when you have many more talents and skills that you could be using. Health issues could be as a direct result of emotional pain from actions or inactions.

Whatever you uncover, please record it in your journal, and consider how you can use this to knowledge and understanding to bring about change and to have fodder for your stories.

TAKE A PERSONAL INVENTORY

Often when you feel stuck in a rut and may hate the job you are in or can't find that one thing you think you are here to do. Adding your personal inventory of skills and talents to your time line is a brilliant way of highlighting how brilliant you really are, but may have forgotten.

Reflect on times of personal achievements or times of personal meaning. Use this list of questions to tease out the talents that you employed at that time.

When (time)

What were you doing?

Emotions you felt?

Talents employed?

How were they employed?

Where were you?

Who were you with?

Pick your top 3 talents from the list above.

Talent

Rank enjoyment

Where used

Where can you use again?

What themes are appearing for you?

Where are the connections?

What does your timeline bring up for you?

What amazing skills or talents do you have?

Jacqui Malpass

ALL ABOUT ME

"To be yourself in a world that is constantly trying to make you something else is the greatest accomplishment."
Unknown

How does examining 'me', help me to discover my healing themes?

Jacqui Malpass

IF I WERE

If I were this necklace

I'd fill the world with miles of bright smiles

And cancel miserable Monday morning faces

Green and Blacks chocolate would be voted a vegetable

And I'd crown Ferdy dog King of the World

If I were this necklace

I'd string together a brighter future

And help everyone reach for the sky

We could all dare to dream, of what we could accomplish

And I'd vote Marmite, the toast topping of choice

If I were this necklace

I'd take away the weekly worry

And everyone would dance on Fridays

Resolutions would be a thing of the past

And I'd make mince pies a regular feast

If were this necklace

I'd wear it with pride

And show the world that I sparkle and glow

A crisp cold Chablis could be the new tea

And laughter & happiness the only way to go

If I were this necklace
I'd make tiramisu just for you
And help you appreciate this wonderful earth
Where goals would be, just for now
And shoes and handbags were given for free

If I were this necklace
I'd share it with you

HOW CAN I REMIND MYSELF WHO I AM?

Life makes memories and memories create stories (and books) and stories change lives. We remind ourselves of who we are by exploring ourselves through journaling and writing. This chapter includes some exercises which are designed to connect you with you and for you to ask the question, 'who am I?'

Before we start digging around in your memory banks, let's start to uncover why you want to journal or write stories and reveal a bit more about who you are and what makes you tick.

Let's start with a few questions, designed to get you thinking about who you are and where your journaling may take you. 5 to 10 minutes on each of these will do, you decide. Date each of your answers, because as you journey through your memory, you will want to come back, reflect, and maybe answer the questions again.

It's fascinating to see how your responses change as you write and reflect.

A LITTLE BIT ABOUT YOU

Who are you?

What is your story?

Why are you journaling / writing?

What is the most important thing you want to discover?

What are the life experiences that make you who you are?

If you were to view your life from an outsider's point of view, what would you know about your life?

Like all exercises, it is best not to think, but to just write.

FRAMING

How you see things affects how you behave. If you see yourself as negative or not having worth then that is what your brain accepts as the truth. Try this 'framing' exercise.

How many I am words or statements can you write? You are NOT allowed to use NOT....

I am kind, caring, intelligent, fun etc...

When you have written them down, head to Wordle www.wordle.net. Copy the words in and play around, print out and turn into a picture. Then frame your drawing and put it up where you can see it every day. Looking at your framed artwork, what does it tell you about who you think you are? It is such a simple yet powerful activity and one which you can repeat often and add to as your idea of who you are changes.

By framing your 'I am' words and placing it somewhere you can see, your brain will also accept those as true.

PHOTOS

Photos are an incredibly powerful way to kick-start your memory. Photos are treasures, moments of your life captured, milestones, birthdays, happy, sad, people long gone, parties you enjoyed, trips, holidays, houses, beaches, there is so much to be captured from your photos and it is not just the picture, it is everything around the photo and, as such, a brilliant way to help you to piece together your life.

The photo journey

Pick a photo, any photo and ask yourself these questions:-

What were you wearing?

Who were you with?

Where were you?

How old were you?

What happened that day?

What happened the day before / day after?

What sounds, smells, and emotions does this bring up?

What else does this memory conjure up?

Describe the place where the photograph was taken.

Describe the other people in the photograph and their relationship to you.

What happened right before this photograph was taken? After?

What surprises you about this picture when that you really look at it?

Who is missing from this picture? Why?

What can't we see in the picture?

If that person in the picture could talk, what would he or she be saying?

VISUALISE MEETING YOU!

Seeing yourself from another's perspective is very powerful and revealing, especially if that other person is you, looking in on you.

You can do this by looking at yourself from a photo and/or from your imagination, describe what you see, as if you had never met yourself. Scary stuff!

From a photograph

Get a recent photograph of yourself. Place the photograph in front of you; now answer these questions. Looking at that person:-

What do you see?

What are you wearing?

What colours do you have on?

What is the style of your clothing, are you dressed for business or leisure?

What is your hairstyle like, your facial expression?

Who else is in the picture with you?

Now imagine that you have never met yourself, write a few paragraphs about the person in the picture. Who do you think they are? Write a bit about their life, hopes, dreams, fears and maybe their perfect day,

From your imagination

Look in the mirror, take a good look. Close your eyes, and when you open them, take a moment and imagine that you are meeting you for the first time.

What is your first impression?

Are you interesting?

Are you a sad or happy person?

What does this person do for a living? What is her/his dream job?

Does she/he have a partner, or children, what are they like?

What is her/his house like?

What other questions do you have? Ask away.

THE STRANGER

We can often learn a lot about ourselves from looking through others eyes. The key is to get inside the strangers skin, become them watching you.

You see yourself sat in a coffee shop, idly drinking your favourite drink and gazing into space. Across the room, a complete stranger is observing you. Write down what they think about you and your life.

THE CLOTHES HANGER

Most of us love clothes. Keep a note of what you wear and how your clothes make you feel, ask yourself why you choose to wear what to do and why. What thoughts do clothes evoke in you?

Your clothes story

Write a short story about a piece of clothing and how it feels, what it sees, hears etc., as if it had human tendencies and were you. Read Green Dress and I in the section of this book called Telling Tales.

PAINT A PICTURE

It is quite fascinating about how we perceive ourselves not only through our thoughts and words but through pictures we take or draw. There are a number of ways you can tackle a piece of reflective art.

Portrait of you

You may not feel like an artist so a stick man or woman will do. Get your pencils or crayons out and start drawing yourself. The drawing can be a combination of colours, words and pictures cut out of magazines.

You can choose some words to describe yourself and make a piece of art around that.

Get skin friendly paints and sponge it all over your face and take a photo.

Keep these creations. What do they tell you? What do you notice about yourself?

FIRSTS

Your life will have many firsts. Your first memory, kiss, fight, book, car, bike, test. Make yourself a list of firsts and then explore where those memories take you.

What is your first memory?

Who did you kiss first?

Who was your first best friend or boyfriend/girlfriend?

First sexual experience?

First marriage, divorce, baby, grandchild?

First holiday, flight, boat trip?

First flat, house, stay away from home?

First death, funeral?

THE DAY THAT CHANGED YOUR LIFE FOREVER

Days which change your life are worth remembering, some may be painful, or gloriously happy, the key is that they changed you in some way. Think what they may be. The day that you left your job and became self-employed. The day someone close died. What happened on the day that your world changed forever. How do these days contribute to who you are and your story?

Think about a significant moment from your life such as a turning point, or a crossroads. Recall the events that led up to that day, what was it about the day that changed your life? Chose a word that signifies that day. Write for 10 minutes about that word and day.

What other days can you write about?

I KNOW THIS STUFF

We know so much more than we give ourselves credit for and often to our own detriment. Ask yourself, how did you manage to get where you are today? That's right; you applied lots of your experience, skills, and knowledge. This is often tied to a lack of self-belief and a lack of confidence.

Your skills might include:-

Communication – the way in which you speak with your friends and family or show how you feel.

Teamwork – the way in which you are ready to muck in and work in collaboration with others.

Leadership – the way in which you motivate and encourage others while taking the lead.

Initiative – the way in which you spot opportunities, set and achieve goals.

Solving problems – your logical or creative thinking which helps you to find solutions to problems.

Flexibility and adaptability – the way in which you have adapted to new situations – what about that time you were chucked in the deep end of a situation and you just got on with it?

Self awareness – knowing your strengths and skills and having the confidence to demonstrate them.

Commitment and motivation – just getting on with what's needed.

Finance – being able to balance the books – paying the bills, saving for nice things, sorting out your credit cards.

What else?

YOU ARE THE EXPERT

Make a list of things you are knowledgeable about.

Evaluate your skills and talents and determine where you are on a scale of one to ten.

If you are not a ten, what has to happen to get you to a ten?

Now that you have a list of your skills write a short bio about yourself.

How could you apply these skills to something you have written about in your journal?

How could you apply these skills to something that happening in a friends life or to a global situation?

If you were to put an advert in the paper offering yourself as an expert, what would your skills be, what would your ad say?

How would you promote yourself?

I AM

If there were just ten words
To say who I was
What would they be?
To wonder who I am
Is profound as to be me
The public self is the one you see
It's the one I know
Or like to show
And when done, who is me?
Is it one of ten words?
Or something quite different?
Without an audience
Who can I be?

Without thinking write down ten words that say who you are. Any ten and in any context. Review and remove until you are left with just one. Circle that one and write 300 words about you and the word.

THE PUBLIC AND PRIVATE YOU

There will always be differences between the private you and the face you show to the public. When someone asks you who are you or what do you do, do you tell them about your job? We often define ourselves by our jobs and roles, when instead it would be more useful to craft a way of saying who you are from your values (read the values exercise in the next chapter) or your ten words.

What have you discovered about you?

What are your ten words and how do they define who you are?

What is your story?

Jacqui Malpass

GETTING FROM VALUES TO VISION

"Every great dream begins with a dreamer. Always remember, you have within you the strength, the patience, and the passion to reach for the stars to change the world."
Harriet Tubman

How do my values, passions and purpose help me to find out what my story is and what stories I want to tell?

You can sit and watch life waft past you like a vague memory or you can be a person who reaches out and shares their gifts. Knowing who you are, understanding your purpose, embracing, and sharing your stories will help you to change and heal your life, and, if you want to eventually write and publish a book, this section will help you find out what it is you want and can share.

First you have to dig deep and find out about you. When you know who you are and what wonderful things you have to share, it makes it easier to start and continue to journal and write. Being very clear about who you are and what you stand for will enable you to have a baseline for you, your life, and your stories.

THE PROCESS OF DISCOVERY

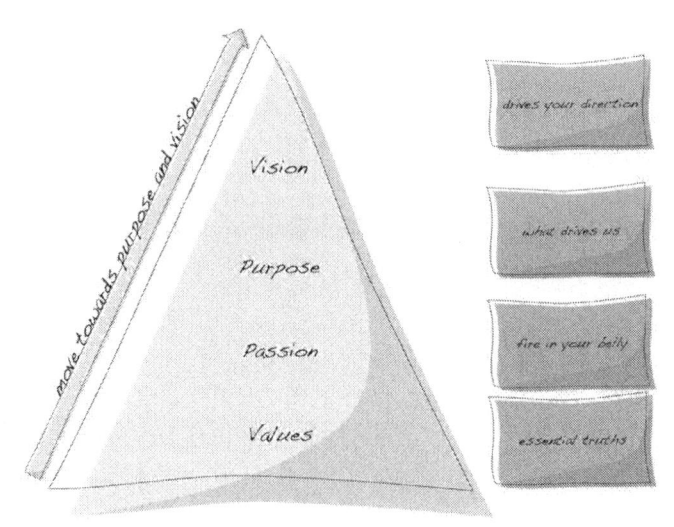

Vision — drives your direction
Purpose — what drives us
Passion — fire in your belly
Values — essential truths
move towards purpose and vision

The process is values, passion, purpose, and vision. Taking steps through the process and working out what your values, passion, and purpose are leads us towards your vision. Without a vision you do not have a direction.

The way I see it is our essential truths create the fire in our bellies and are what drives us as humans. When you know your purpose (mission) you can create a vision for the future and this will drive the direction in which you go. When you **have clarity** you can define where you are headed with your life.

Imagine your life is a book and you are discovering what that book is about.

Imagine if your journal was to become a book of your life – your memoir even. You are going to become your reader, trying to understand you and your life. Your readers will have expectations. Your role as a journaler and writer, is to make sure those expectations are met, while at the same time fulfilling the purpose of your journaling and writing.

WHAT DO I HAVE TO SAY?

After you have decided to write in a journal or create stories, often what happens is that your clarity fades, self-doubt rushes in and you start to wonder what was it you wanted to say. There are three statements that may resonate with you:-

I have nothing to say.

I think I have something to say, but I am not sure what.

I know I have something to say, but not how.

WHAT MIGHT I WANT TO SAY?

Try some free writing. Don't worry about spelling, grammar or sentence structure. The only rule is that once you begin writing, you continue until the time is up.

Before I start to write I sit in silence, sometimes closing my eyes and focusing on my breath. You will be amazed, how it all flows once you start and the most important thing for me is that, even if it is only one sentence, that's all it needs to be. All of this self-doubt, overwhelm and mind clutter is normal. The process will help you to declutter.

Grab a pen and paper, close your eyes, and remember to breathe, focus inwards and start writing. What I want to share with myself about my life story is...

WHAT DO PEOPLE ASK ME ABOUT?

There will be something that you always get asked about. What do your friends, family and colleagues come to you for? What kind of advice do you hear yourself imparting, time and time again. What experiences do you regularly share? This should give you some clues about who you are, your values, passions, purpose and mission.

WHAT HAS HAPPENED IN MY LIFE I NEED TO LET GO OF?

We all have stuff and I find that writing creative life stories, prose and poetry, helps to move things on.

What stuff do you want to let go of? Who do you want to distance yourself from? What if you could change the way your story ends?

Go through the values to vision exercises as is you were writing a book of your life.

VALUES

Values are ways of being that mean something important to you. Your values are the qualities that you want to present to the world. They are what you believe are important. They are the foundations of who you are.

Values are those things that you come back to, which tell you that your life is going in the right direction. The number that you have is not important. What is important is that you know what they are. They can change as your life changes.

For example beauty, to me, means seeing the inner beauty of others, not the outward plastic means nothing self-obsession that parades in front of me.

I rarely see what people look like on the outside until they highlight it to me. What I see is the inner being whose qualities shine through.

Discovering your values

Once you are clear on your values you can move towards them. Once your mind can visualise them and you believe them, your mind, being very clever, will just know what they are. Run through the next exercise twice, once to discover your primary values and second to discover your values for another part of your life. They may be the same or different.

Quickly write 30 words that mean something to you.

Group them so that similar words are together. Keep these and reflect later on what they may mean to you.

Next, be brutal and whittle your list down to just eight.

Next to each value write about why it is important to you.

When you understand your own values, you can use them to make decisions about how to live your life, run your business, which career your choose, relationships with others, and a whole host of other things. You will then be able to answer questions such as:-

What business should I be in?

What career path should I pursue?

Should I start my own business?

Should I stay in this relationship?

What compromises am I willing to make?

Should I follow what others expect or go with my heart?

Staying connected with your values is an on-going lifetime exercise. As you change so will your values. Really take the time to understand your values and the real priorities in your life, from

Writing to Heal

there you will be able to set your direction and stick to what you believe in and are passionate about.

PASSION

Your passion is what will shine through your journaling and writing. You may not be clear on what that is yet, in which case the next section will help you to uncover what you are passionate about. You may be passionate about many things, when you write in your journal these will start to become clear and when you write your stories, you will be writing about what you care about and which really resonate with you.

What are you good at, or have a natural aptitude for, which you love doing? Not what are you good at but hate.

When you were a child, what did you love to do?

When you are lost in time, what are you doing?

Who or what are you envious of?

Thinking of the last time someone said your eyes lit up when you were talking. What were you talking about?

If everything you were passionate about was going to be taken away and you only had 30 seconds to make a list, what would be on your list?

If there was nothing standing in your way, what would you be doing?

If money were no object what would you do every day?

If you could learn anything and it was fun, what would you learn?

Who or what inspires you?

When you're sitting in front of your computer what do you research the most?

Imagine you are sitting with a friend, what you talk about the most; what lights you up?

Look at your bookcase, which books interest you the most?

What are the problems that others face that you find really easy to sort out?

If you had a gift for the world what would it be?

Write what I am passionate about is…

PURPOSE

Our purpose is what drives us, gets us up each day, and is our mission in life.

> **"Writing or reviewing a mission statement changes you because it forces you to think through your priorities deeply, carefully, and to align your behaviour with your beliefs."**
>
> (Covey 2004)

The purpose of your journal and your stories is to help you to heal and, if you decide to share to help others, to imagine **what is possible for them** from what you have discovered.

Writing about areas of your life and subjects that fire you up, which are aligned with your values, is so much more fun than dreary ones that leave you cold and unmotivated.

Imagine again that writing this book about your life is your dream. Finding your purpose will lead to a purposeful story or book, or one that has a purpose.

A purpose led story or book is one that is written from your heart, it has meaning to you and to those that you share it with. Your purpose is your way of sharing your message based on what you are passionate about.

Each of us has a purpose, something which we are here to deliver and as our lives unfold, our knowledge grows and deepens, and then opportunities for our purpose open up.

It is about being connected to our authentic self, the one which is most creative, intuitive, passionate, links to the big picture, values based, and is what we love doing without thinking.

Many people feel disharmony and frustration because they 'still haven't found what they are looking for.' They try many things and head down lots of blind avenues searching for the thing, when usually and very often it is right under their noses. Even when someone does find their purpose, obstacles appear, and choices are made which can also lead to frustration because we feel we are not fulfilling our purpose. When you live your life on purpose the bumps you encounter are just little blips on the journey.

Purpose may appear out of tragedy or adversity, it may appear on holiday, or when you suddenly decide to pack it all in and head home, it may appear in a song or poem or you may consciously will it into being.

I believe the bumps are designed to help us grow and become clear and I also believe that something like writing in a journal is a great catalyst for exploring your options. When you write with purpose, your writing will flow, and you will feel a deep connection to it.

Steps to creating your purpose statement:

List the action words that you connect with, e.g. educate, accomplish, empower, encourage, improve, help, give, guide, inspire, integrate, master, motivate, nurture, organise, produce, promote, travel, spread, share, satisfy, understand, teach, write, etc.

List everything and everyone that you believe you can help, e.g. people, creatures, organisations, causes, groups, environment, etc.

Who do you really want to help?

What is the result of you helping your who?

What will it be possible for others to achieve or do as a result of you changing your life and / or reading your stories?

What is your purpose?

YOUR PERSONAL VISION

Vision drives your direction; it is future based and relies on you taking action to get you there. Your vision then is something that will propel you towards things that you want to achieve in the future.

Your personal vision statement is a **written description of your future desired life** as seen in your mind's eye. There is no right format or length, however the more detailed and specific your vision is, the more connected to you it will be, and the easier it will be to set your outcomes or goals.

Craft your vision statement

Take your values, passion, and purpose and design a meaningful statement. Write in the first person and make statements about the future you wish to achieve. Be specific about what you want to achieve, set a time frame, and articulate the statements in such a way that they can be evaluated and measured.

Use the PACER, well-formed outcomes model to help you.

OUTCOMES

Remember Alice in Wonderland. Alice, lost, comes across the Cheshire Cat:

"Excuse me sir," Alice enquires, "could you tell me which road to take?"

Wisely the cat asks, "Where are you going?"

Somewhat dismayed, Alice responds, "Oh, I don't know where I'm going sir."

"Well," replied the cat, "if you don't know where you are going, it really doesn't matter which road you take."

Take a step back and look at the big picture and consider what your outcome is. Instead of rushing into the doing, take a little time and plan your journey.

Having a roadmap is not the key to a successful life; it is the key to helping to make the journey easier. Having a clearly defined destination will help you achieve your outcomes.

Habit 2: begin with the end in mind
(Covey 2004)

Covey asks 'Are you--right now--who you want to be, what you dreamed you'd be, doing what you always wanted to do? Be honest. Sometimes people find themselves achieving victories that are empty--successes that have come at the expense of things that were far more valuable to them. If your ladder is not leaning against the right wall, every step you take gets you to the wrong place faster.

Habit 2 is based on imagination--*the ability to envision in your mind what you cannot at present see with your eyes. It is based on the principle that all things are created twice. There is a mental (first) creation, and a physical (second) creation. The physical creation follows the mental, just as a building follows a blueprint. If you don't make a conscious effort to visualize who you are and what you want in life, then you empower other people and circumstances to shape you and your life by default. It's about connecting again with your own uniqueness and then defining the personal, moral, and ethical guidelines within which you can most happily express and fulfil yourself. Begin with the End in Mind means to begin each day, task, or project with a clear vision of your desired direction and destination, and then continue by flexing your proactive muscles to make things happen.*

The end is the outcome. To get the most out of any situation you need to focus on the outcome that you want to achieve. When we know what the outcome (our vision) is, we can plan the journey.

Outcome (noun)

1. a final product or end result; consequence; issue.

2. a conclusion reached through a process of logical thinking.

http://dictionary.reference.com/browse/outcome

In the context of well-formed outcomes, they are positive things and provide a sense of well-being and positive emotion. If the outcome is not positive, then I would question the value and validity of it. If it makes you feel unhappy, then change it. We want to create a positive causal link to a positive end result.

The difference between where we are (current status) and where we want to be (the outcome) is what we do (action).

PACER

Instead of SMART goals, I use the NLP model PACER for setting well-formed outcomes. It is an alternative way of thinking about what you want to achieve.

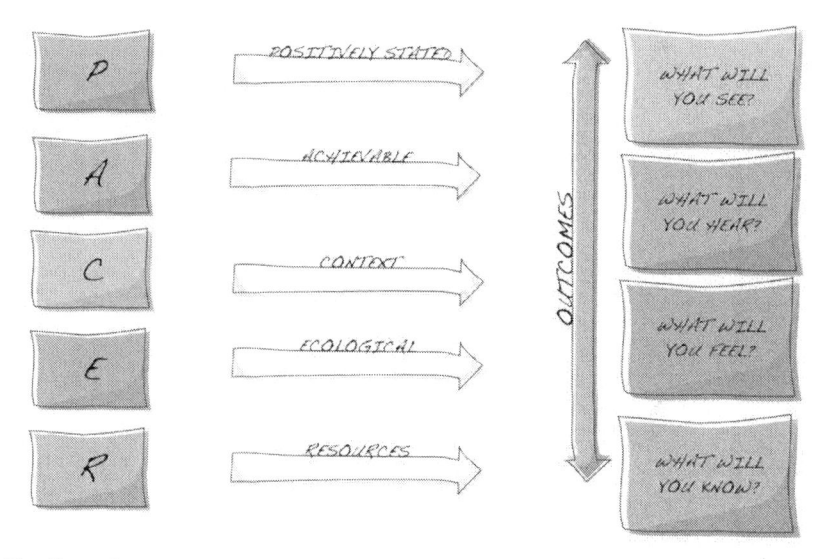

P — POSITIVELY STATED
A — ACHIEVABLE
C — CONTEXT
E — ECOLOGICAL
R — RESOURCES

OUTCOMES:
- WHAT WILL YOU SEE?
- WHAT WILL YOU HEAR?
- WHAT WILL YOU FEEL?
- WHAT WILL YOU KNOW?

By focusing on outcomes, we are not looking at and end goal, we are looking at a how we create our desired outcomes and then keeping them firmly focused in our minds, whilst remembering that the journey towards an outcome is rarely in a straight line.

Using PACER, I want to ask, what is your vision? What steps will take you towards a new and positive reality which brings the book of your new life into being?

P – Positively stated

The human mind is unable to process the word 'not' at an unconscious level. Ever been told not to do something and then had a compulsion to do it? So if your outcome is set in the negative "I am NOT going to eat chocolate," the mind will make the association "I AM going to eat chocolate". When setting your outcome, make it something that you will work positively toward rather than something you should avoid.

Instead of 'I am sick of my boring life, think 'I am working towards creating a new life.

A – Achievable

Ask yourself, is your outcome achievable?

How will you achieve it?

How will you know when you have succeeded?

How will you measure your progress?

When thinking about achievement, focus on the sensory evidence that will tell you that you've succeeded.

What will you see, hear, feel or know?

C – Context

Context means situation or circumstances, if you are writing a story it will mean the setting. When defining our outcome we need to base it in our 'own reality'. We want an outcome that is real, tangible and to stand a chance of success we need to believe **success is within our reach.** Context needs to define with whom, where and when you want this outcome.

Where do you want your outcome?

With whom do you want it?

When do you want it? (What is the time frame for this outcome?)

E – Ecological

Think about who might be affected by your outcomes and how they will feel. You might find that you may have to give up something in order to achieve what you want. There may also be underlying unconscious considerations to contemplate. Ask yourself these 4 questions:-

If you get this outcome, what **will** you have?

If you get this outcome, what **won't** you have?

If you **do not** get this outcome, what **will** you have?

If you **do not** get this outcome, what **won't** you have?

R – Resources

Resources are the things that will help you to achieve your outcomes, they may be within you, be help from others or things that you can utilise. If you don't ask you won't get!

Ask yourself what you need within yourself, including the qualities and skills that you already have or may need in the future?

What resources do you already have in terms of time, materials, people, and money?

What resources can you acquire, and from where and whom?

Do you need any new resources in terms of skills or behaviours for yourself or others?

And finally... Check the effects of achieving your outcomes.

Having achieved your outcome, how does it affect you?

How else does it affect you...?

And what does that mean for you?

What are the effects on other people – friends, family, work colleagues, etc.?

What other effects might there be and what are the implications?

What would your time commitment be?

How much effort is required?

How much money do you need to invest?

Evidence

Your outcome may be to change a relationship, career, find something you enjoy doing, it may be to write and publish the book of your life, or it may be to create a new income stream. Ask yourself:-

How will you know that you have achieved your outcome?

Ask yourself what will you see, hear, and feel? What will others see, hear, and feel?

Responsibility

You have set your outcome, now it is your responsibility to bring it alive.

Grab a pen and some post it notes and ask...

What is your outcome?

What do I have to do to reach my outcome?

What are your eight values?
What is your personal vision?
What are your well formed outcomes?
What is driving you to journal and write?
What is the vision for the book of your life?

Jacqui Malpass

Writing to Heal

WRITING EXERCISES

"And by the way, everything in life is writable about if you have the outgoing guts to do it, and the imagination to improvise. The worst enemy to creativity is self-doubt."
Charlotte Bronte

Writing prompts to help you get started.

We often get stuck when we put pen to paper, so these prompts are designed to help inspire you.

DAYS

These are days that really stick in your mind; ask yourself why, what did you learn, what are you grateful for, how do you get more of these days?

Days writing exercises

Days when 'that' happens I…

My first 10 days of…

The best day of my life was…

If you were to bury a time capsule of today what would go in it?

DREAMS

I believe that dreams are metaphors for emotional release. They are messages for us to unravel and interpret. Because we are all unique we must look inwards to try to work out what our dreams and dream symbols mean to us.

Immediately on waking - Write down or draw what you remember from your dream. Leave it for at least 24 hours and then come back and break it down, working out what each element means to you. Ask yourself, what do you think the message is?

Our brains constantly look for patterns and matching experiences, so that you may see something in a dream such as your mum, but that could just be a representation of an older female or someone who is motherly or whatever personality traits your mum exhibits.

It has to be said I have the strangest dreams. However, for me, capturing my dreams is an essential part of my daily life. I look at the symbols inside the dreams, rather than the story of the dream. These are my symbols and not symbols from a dream book. I record my dreams and then come back to look at them sometime later to try to understand what the message is.

For example, I recently dreamt that I was in bed with a person with whom I had had poor business dealings and they were covered in oil, very smooth and brown. My interpretation was - to be careful of whom my business bedfellows are, as there are some slippery characters to be wary of.

The reason why all dream content is metaphorical and not directly about 'real life' is that the brain cannot generate the 'real world'. All of our senses are switched off whilst we are dreaming, so the brain looks for patterns internally, drawing on memories that resonate emotionally and then provides a story for us to interpret.

This is why dreams often seem so odd; they draw on memories and images from your entire life. Therefore, every person you see in a dream is standing in metaphorically for someone else in real life.

THE BANK OF GREAT THOUGHTS AND FEELINGS

This is a lovely exercise; you create for yourself a bank of thoughts and feelings; stuff that makes you feel really good to be alive. Then in your odd moments when you're feeling a little down, you can go back to your bank and feelings and use them to lift your spirits by writing something inspired by them.

What's in your bank?

Start by writing a series of single words, for example: – Sunrise / Smile / Chocolate / Walk / Wine / Breeze / Kiss. You get the idea.

Take one of your words, what is the best experience you can recall about that particular word?

Take a moment and close your eyes what can you see, feel, hear, what colours do you see, what smells are there, who was with you, what did they all you say, what or who else was there?

What is the story around that word?

LETTERS

Do you keep old letters? These are a brilliant way to piece together parts of your life. For each letter put them in chronological order, reread them, making notes of what comes to mind.

Find significant letters and add photos or objects that you still have. Use these to form a letter journal.

Perhaps you could write a letter back to each of those people, knowing what you know now.

30 days, 30 letters

30 days of letters to your most important people. If you haven't kept letters, simply start your own collection and write to the people in your life or who have touched your life.

ENCHANTED RELATIONSHIPS

Choose two or three of your closest relationships, it may be a friend, a lover / partner or parent.

Who are they?

Why are they your closest relationships?

What do you love about them the most?

YOUR FAN CLUB

Who's a part of your fan club? Journal about the people who support you unconditionally. How have they helped you? How do you value them? Keep a record as they do something wonderful.

Whose fan club are you a part of? As someone says thank you or asks you for your advice, keep a record. You are in their fan club.

This is your chance to give back for all the fabulous support you've been given.

Being part of a community helps us accomplish so much more than we could alone. It's important to nurture these communities and keep them strong.

Don't forget to say thank you to your fan club!

WHAT OTHERS ARE SAYING

Keep a log of things that people say about you.

Date.

Person.

Relationship to you.

What they said.

How you felt.

You may be surprised at how many positive things people say that we choose to ignore. Why do we do that?

A SINGLE WORD

Ask a selection of people to choose a single word that describes you.

Write a character sketch of yourself using these words.

AROUND THE HOUSE

Wander around your house, looking at your clothes, shoes, handbags, open the fridge, and look at the things you like to eat, what's on the wine rack, describe your lounge, or bedroom. Write a sketch of the person you have just discovered. What does this tell you?

PEOPLE TYPES

Thinking about the people that you meet, have some fun, and put them into categories:-

Lovers.

Friends.

Strangers.

Heroes.

Villains.

Snobs.

Animals.

Children.

Colleagues.

What does this tell you about these people?

Examine your relationships.

What stories can you make up with the people in your life, write about them in these roles?

WHO ARE THESE PEOPLE?

There is usually someone, other than you, at the heart of every story. Who are they? This next exercise gives you a great opportunity to understand someone better. Imagine that you are interviewing someone who intrigues you. Answer these questions.

How old are they?

Male or female?

Happy?

How would their friends describe them?

How would their enemies describe them?

Do they have children?

What do they do for a living?

What other career did they have?

What is the best thing that happened to them?

What is the worst thing that happened to them?

Are they political?

Do they anything they are passionate about?

Distinguishing feature?

Educated?

What are they proudest of having achieved?

Any skeletons in the closet?

What food do they hate?

What last made them cry?

If you were to put them into a people type category, what would they be?

Ask them to solve a problem or issue, see it through their eyes, feel what they feel, say it like they would.

What does this tell you about this person?

What does it say about you?

What have you learnt?

MY HERO / HEROINE WOULD

Imagine someone from your favourite film or book. These can be superheroes with amazing qualities.

What are their special qualities?

How do they solve their problems?

Thinking of an issue you want to resolve, look at it through the eyes of your hero or heroine.

How would they solve your problem?

What advice do they give you?

How can you now solve your problem?

You can repeat this exercise using another of your people types, for example, imagine a snob looking at your problem, what would they say and do? What about a wolf man?

POSTCARD TO SELF

Places like Vista print (www.vistaprint.co.uk) and other online printing outlets often make offers of free postcards. Get yourself 100 free postcards printed with something funky on the front and every once in a while send yourself a postcard.

You can write anything on your postcard and when it turns up a few days later do whatever the postcard asks you to do. E.g. make something you have never eaten before, like raw chocolates.

Jacqui Malpass

Writing to Heal

REFLECTING

"Sleep on your writing: take a walk over it; scrutinise it of a morning; review it of an afternoon; digest it after a meal; let it sleep in your drawer a twelve month; never venture a whisper about it to your friend, if he be an author especially." Robert Benchley

How does reflection help me to write stories and start to heal?

Reflection is our response to experiences, situations, events or new information and a phase where processing and learning can take place. When you reflect your unconscious mind searches for evidence and analyses it. After which it tries to make meaning and draw conclusions based on the evidence presented. Once we have been able to evaluate what we are reflecting on, we can then decide what's next.

Reflection is a powerful learning experience. We learn and process as we write. Reflection allows us to further process so that we can make meaning of our words, make changes, and start the healing process.

In order to make sense of our writing, we simply have to leave it. Reflective thinking is about going back and looking at your journal, analysing what you have written, with the goal of making decisions about what to do or what not to do and being able to find the inspiration for your stories.

In learning to change your behaviour you must first define the problem to solve – the things you are writing about. Journaling and reflecting is a problem solving strategy. Remember that "learning" is the goal and the "problem" (journaling) is a method for learning.

Reflection is simply a process which enables you to make meaning from your writing, challenge your thinking, learn who you are and gives you the opportunity to make choices about changing the way you behave.

What stops us growing and changing is us. Change happens when we stop repeating our habitual patterns and behaviours and begin to see things in a new way and, in the process, discover the power to create the results we want.

The best decisions come, when we can step away from our problems and take time to think. Of course in the fast paced life that we lead, making time to think is seen as a luxury.

My thinking time comes when I walk my dog, take a swim, chop the veg, stand in the shower, luxuriate in the bath or overnight as I sleep. Things really do seem clearer in the morning or after a long walk.

When you reflect you are looking for linkages, common points of reference and those aha moments. Images and emotions stored in your long term memory will come to mind to help.

For me it is a combination of logic and creativity.

Journaling, writing stories and books has changed my life. It's not always easy, but it has really helped to put things into perspective.

HOW DO I REFLECT?

Reflection does not mean sitting in the lotus position omming, though of course you could. Reflection has a few basic elements:-

Retelling- state the basic facts (write a journal entry) and consider how you felt about it at the time and how you feel about it now.

Examine – examine and relate the feelings or events to other times when you have felt the same way.

Reflecting – How do you change your behaviours? What possible alternatives, perspectives, meanings, or links can you see?

SIMPLE REFLECTION

Simple reflection comes from taking any of your journal entries and completing the following questions.

Describe the situation.

What did I do? What happened? What did I say?

Who was with me?

How well or not so well did it go?

How do I think or feel about it?

What did I think about but not say?

What did I learn?

What will I do differently next time?

How will I do it differently next time?

What have I achieved?

What have I learnt about myself?

LEARNING TO STAND BACK AND BEING OUT OF THE PICTURE

Sometimes when you write about painful experiences, you start to relive the experience, which may be unhelpful. It is important to get this stuff out and on to paper.

Once we have done that, it is even more important that, when we reflect on it, we do so from a stand back position and to remain out of the picture, so that we can view it objectively and without emotion.

Writing to Heal

We take a stand back / out of the picture position, so that it protects it from the pain we may have been feeling, it separates feeling from the images that we can see, it allows us to see the event in a new way and therefore put it to bed.

Out of the picture reflection

Take one of your journal entries and write it on a piece of paper.
Place the paper on the floor.
Standing looking at the paper and journal entry, reflect on the situation.
Look at it from a distance and think about how you might resolve it or change it.

IN THE PICTURE

When we reflect on something that was great it is better to reflect when we are in the picture so that we can remember, see, feel and hear all of the great things that happened. You can use these positive experiences whenever you are feeling down.

In the picture reflection

Take one of your journal entries and write it on a piece of paper.
This needs to be about something good and positive.
Place the paper on the floor.
Standing on the paper and journal entry, reflect on the situation.
Close your eyes. Let all of the great feelings wash over you.

THE POWER OF I STATEMENTS

Use "I" statements. Review and look for journal entries that say things like 'he / she made me…'. You are looking to change the 'he made me', to, 'I felt' or 'I did or said'.

For example 'he /she made me so mad, when I walked through the door and saw the pile of dishes, once again piled up and he / she was sitting on the sofa drinking tea.' Could be changed to I felt so angry when…. After which you can examine why it made you angry and what has to happen to change your feelings. You are looking at how you can take ownership for your feelings and reactions.

WHERE AND WHEN TO REFLECT

You can reflect anywhere, anytime; walking, sitting on the bus, driving, munching your lunch, staring out to sea, in the bath… Go with your natural instinct and flow. If you have developed a ritual, go with it.

COLOUR CODING

You may want to consider using some kind of highlighting system for things you want to concentrate on. Colour is really effective and will catch your eye when you go back and forth through your journal.

YOUR ACTIONS

This book is a learning tool and should be used to help you with your on-going process for continuous improvement, where the real learning comes when you let your unconscious mind process what you have been reflecting and journaling on.

You will very probably find that when you come back to something you have written, you will get an amazing aha moment.

Change comes from within you and is so much more powerful when you see it in black and white and you have **chosen to reflect**, discover, learn new behaviours, and **put what you have learnt about you into action**.

How do you like to reflect?

When will you reflect?

How will you record your reflections for change, healing, and stories?

Jacqui Malpass

REFLECTION EXERCISES

"If I don't write to empty my mind, I go mad." Lord Byron

It is in reflection that comes clarity. More exercises to help you discover what your journaling and writing is telling you.

In addition to the other journaling and writing exercises, dotted throughout this book these additional reflection exercises are designed to do just that, to get you thinking about your thinking.

THOUGHT REPORT

The thought report is for recording one off incidents, where you want some clarity. For example something may have happened in work, which triggered a reaction in you. These are sometimes unpleasant experiences that you would like to have handled differently. You can also write about past or current experiences.

Think of a situation that you want to review and reflect on. Go though each of these.

Situation – describe the situation you found yourself in.

Emotions – describe the emotions you felt, both positive and negative.

Thoughts – what thoughts came into your head, both positive and negative?

Evidence – what evidence do you have both for and against the events? Have you been in a similar situation before? What strengths do you bring to this situation? Make sure you see the whole picture.

Alternatives – now that you have considered the facts, what is a different, healthier way to view the situation?

Learn – what have you learned about you and others? What will you do next time?

What will you now do differently?

AT THE MOVIES

Think back to an entry in your journal, which may have been an unpleasant event. As you start to reread the event, imagine that what you have written is a script for a play.

Picture a movie screen in front of you and watch the characters in your play act out the event.

Remember to stay out of the picture (experience). You are a moviegoer sitting comfortably in a chair looking up at the screen and you have the advantage of seeing the situation from everybody's perspective.

What do you notice about how each character is acting, that you didn't notice when you wrote the original journal entry?

What do you notice about what each character is saying?

How could the problem have been averted?

What advice would you give to each of the characters?

What did you learn?

As you think about the experience and what you have just seen and heard, you now have the benefit of hindsight, ask yourself these questions:-

What would you like to have happened instead?

How could you have behaved differently?

Now rewrite the script. Write out what you will be doing differently next time.

Now that you have a new script for your play, start to run the play upon the movie screen in front of you, only this time you are taking part. See the play through your own eyes, hear what you want to hear, and act the way that you would have liked to have acted, and achieve the results you really wanted.

Blank screen, rerun the movie, and do this at least 10 times.

Rewrite the script from other people's perspectives. Run this through on your movie screen.

What did you learn?

BUILDING ON SUCCESS

Looking back through your journal, pick a time that something went really well for you. Make a note of the great things that happened, the feelings that you felt and what you saw and heard. What led up to that event and what followed it?

Put the movie up on the screen, remembering to put you in the leading role. Take yourself back into the situation, see it through your own eyes and feel all those great feelings again.

What do you notice about the contribution that you made to your success?

What exactly did you do to make it a success?

How many other situations are there, where you have made something of a great success?

What did each of those situations have in common?

Thinking about those behaviours, how could you use them again, more successfully, in the future?

Thinking about a situation that is coming up, write a short piece focusing on the outcome that you would like to achieve and using all of the behaviours that you know work for successful situations. Run it through the movie exercise. How does that feel?

TRIGGERS

Take one of your triggers, the things that push your buttons. You have a choice in how to react to situations. If you know your buttons are being pushed, check your reaction immediately, examine your thoughts, consider your body talk, focus on your breathing, and make a choice to do something differently.

Flipping the emotional switch from self-defeating patterns and feelings to those that serve you better can take time, practice, and patience.

Triggers are products of some past event. Remember that the situation is not happening now. Try to trace back to the first time that this trigger occurred, how many similar events can you remember?

Pick a trigger, one that you know without fail, sparks something in you.

What happened just before the event?

What did you see, hear, feel, smell, or taste?

Stand back from the drama, what do you notice?

What other occasions has this triggered this behaviour?

What can you identify as the root cause?

What would you advise yourself to do differently?

How could you change the picture into a positive experience?

What advice would you give yourself?

How will you take responsibility for changing your responses?

WALK THE LINE

We all have a strategy for dealing with and re-presenting time. We have to have a way of knowing the difference between past, present and future, otherwise how would we know the difference?

To consider how you organise time, first think of something in your past, and notice the direction the thought came from. Now think of something in the future and again, notice the direction. Now point to the past and the future to gain a sense of your personal time-line.

Your perception may align with one of the two major orientations, which in NLP (neuro-linguistic programming) are called through time (experience life in a continuum) or in time (time is now) – or you may be a combination of both.

In Timers tend to indicate a left-right line just in front of them. Through Timers will point forwards and backwards and gesture towards themselves for 'now'. But don't worry if it's not as clear as that for you.

In-time - Having a time line with 'now" passing through your body.

Through time – The line is outside your body. It often has the past on one side and the future on the other.

What does this mean to you as a journaler and writer?
Through Time

Through Time people like lists, are good at making plans, knowing what steps to take, can easily imagine taking the steps to where they want to be, and stick to them. You may plan incessantly what you will be doing in the future and may go through a long process before making a decision (do a procrastination action plan!). You are likely to be on time for appointments and will be meticulous in keeping a diary. Which is great news for setting and getting into good habits, like making writing time and keeping a journal.

In Time

In Time people don't want lists or to be tied down in any way. You will live 'for the moment', can easily get caught up in the 'here and now', forget you have a book to write or write and forget you have a life to live. You may have difficulty planning because of lack of awareness of the future. You may not finish what you start. You will find a coach invaluable as they will hold you accountable.

Being able to switch to *through time* is a useful skill to have for managing and finding time to journal and write. Recognising which you typically are will enable you to devise some strategies so that you manage your time more effectively.

Walk the line exercise

In this exercise you will be laying out events, issues, or problems on a timeline and then looking for patterns from a distance so that you can gain perspective.

Step 1

You will need paper and post-it notes.

Get 3 pieces of paper and write; now, past and future, put these in a line on the floor.

Think of a recent event when something happened and your buttons were pressed. Write this on a post-it note and put it on the past sheet.

Remember to date all of your events, as far as you can.

What other times did the same thing happen? Write these down and add them to the past sheet.

When was the very first time that it happened? Add a date to this event and put it on the past sheet.

Put them in chronological order.

Using post-its - brainstorm these past events – looking for patterns.

Where were you?

Who were you with?

What were the events leading up to the event?

What was the trigger?

What did you do, hear, say, or feel?

What happened next?

Add any other thoughts and feelings onto post-it notes and place them on the timeline alongside the events.

Stand back and reflect on them, where are the repeating patters?

Step 2

Create a set of post-its for how you would like to react next time one of these triggers or buttons is pushed.

Lay them on your future time line; you can link them to events or specific triggers.

Stand back and reflect, what else might you need?

Writing to Heal

Write up your strategy for handling these in the future.

[Diagram: A timeline with "Past" on the left showing boxes labeled "first event", "event", "event", "recent event", then "Now", then "Future" on the right with "next time" and four "I will" boxes. Below the past side: "look for patterns". Below the future side: "create new strategies".]

Step 3

Next, you need a bag. A rubbish bag of some sort - this can be imaginary or real.

Step 4

Go to the very first past event. Stand back and observe this and each of the events, thinking of how you would have liked each event to turn out, with the new strategies you have on your future timeline.

Pick up every event in turn and put it in your rubbish bag.

When you get to the end of the line, decide what you want to do with your rubbish bag - burn it, jump on it, shred it - these are all now well and truly behind you.

Step 5

Look at your future line and read all of the new behaviours that you want to adopt. Reflect on what else might you want to add?

Walk onto your future timeline, step onto each of your new behaviours, stand still, and feel everything associated with your new way of thinking and behaving.

Note what you see, feel, hear as you let the words associated with your new behaviours wash over you.

TALKING TIME

You can understand how you manage time by the language that you use. You may for example say this *has* been a problem, this *is* a problem, or this *will* be a problem. And before I can or after I have done. You also use expressions that describe how you experience time and where your timeline is:-

Time is on my side.

You should put it behind you.

Looking ahead there is a brighter future.

It was in the dim and distant past.

I'm looking forward to a holiday.

I am going to write a book / I am writing my book.

Look back at your journaling and writing, which of these do you notice? Take a journal entry and rewrite your entry putting the incident / issue behind you, e.g.

I just know that it will be a real problem when I go to Mari with the sales figures.

When I go to Mari with the sales figures I will have looked at what the problems were and found a way to address them.

STAYING ON TRACK - INTERNAL VS. EXTERNAL LOCUS OF CONTROL

People draw their motivation from different sources, their external world or from within themselves.

Those with an *Internal Locus of Control* get their motivation from inside themselves and reference themselves to see have well they are performing.

What happens to them, they feel, is as a direct result of their actions. They will create a set of criteria and judge how well they are doing against them.

Those with an *External Locus of Control* are motivated by feedback from the outside world. What happens to them is a result of what other people or events do to them. They are influenced by others and may experience inertia or overwhelm until someone is available to guide them in the right direction.

To identify internal or external LOC, the easiest way is to ask yourself, 'How do you know when you have written a good report / journal entry/ story / book?' Someone with an internal LOC may look at you slightly confused and say 'I just know' or tell you about the criteria they selected and judged themselves against. Internals also say 'I think' a lot and point to themselves when answering a question. By contrast, someone with an external LOC will answer with reference to other peoples view or opinion.

Look through some of your journal entries and ask if you have been validating yourself through others or if you are confident about your own decisions.

Choose a journal entry and write a short piece as if you were the opposite way to your normal way of being. For example if you find that you constantly refer to your partner or a friend when making a decision, write about how you decided that you would do something.

THE CARROT OR THE STICK - AWAY FROM OR TOWARDS MOTIVATIONS

What motivates people to getting things done can also be affected by something called towards or away from motivations. These can change depending upon which area of your life you are thinking about.

Away from people think in terms of what should be avoided and are energised by threats, 'if I don't finish this then I will never be an author'. They tend to procrastinate and won't do something until it becomes really painful, then they tend to rush, making mistakes and getting stressed because it all becomes too difficult. They find sticking to goals hard, but are good at sorting through their mess.

Towards people think in terms of positive outcomes and goals and are motivated by achievement: 'If I finish this book and get it published, I will be able to use it to improve my life and help others'. They can easily imagine the future, but may set unrealistic goals, like planning four books when they should just focus on one.

Strategies

Find out which you are by asking what is important to you about changing and healing your life. Consider your language, is it positive or negative, are you thinking about positive reference points or avoiding problems? Towards people tend to say 'enjoy' 'gain' 'get' and 'achieve', whilst away from people will say 'avoid' 'fix' 'prevent' and 'don't ...'

Are you moving towards positive outcomes or are you moving away from negatives outcomes?

There is no right or wrong approach; you might be towards or away from in different contextual situations. For example, you may be hugely towards in work, and very away from in personal relationships.

Let's start by asking a few questions:-

What do you look for in a relationship? You could also choose friendship, buying a new computer, selecting a great holiday.

Write down at least three things that you look for and write them in your language.

Looking at what you have written, now ask yourself the following question, why is (and insert exactly what you have written) important to you?

Do this for each of your three answers.

Now let's consider your answers. Have you said things like, 'I like it when...', or have you written things like, 'I don't want', 'I don't like', 'I hate', 'I need to get away from people who are like...'?

Rewrite your sentences in a way that is opposite to how you have written them, how does that feel?

By looking closely at what you've written you will see very clearly whether you are a towards or away from type of person.

By knowing this you will know how to motivate yourself to achieve your outcomes.

You may also get a good idea, of how the people around you are motivated and may start to understand why there is a possible mismatch of communication between you.

OBSTACLES

Have you ever wondered why you constantly put obstacles in your way? How often do you catch yourself saying 'I can't do this because...'? 'I would have done it but...' 'I would love to do that but I don't know how...'

Think of something that would really like to do, now write a list all the reasons why you can't do it.

Now pick three of those things and start to write, how, if you had everything you needed to have, you would actually overcome those obstacles?

When you look at your writing how often do you notice that you are selling yourself short, highlighting the failures, or telling yourself or others that you simply can't do something?

The more often you tell them the more often they will believe it, and of course, so will you.

YOUR SENSES

The VAK (visual, auditory, kinaesthetic) model from NLP describes how we re-present the outside world to ourselves. Understanding others preferred VAK model, will help you to develop yourself so that you can engage with other people who typically think and make meaning in another sense to you.

These senses are:

Visual-seeing

Auditory-hearing

Kinaesthetic-feeling

Olfactory-smelling

Gustatory-tasting

Spiritual-intuition

Go back and look at your journal entries and notice what sensory language you use when you write. Now try to rewrite the sentences in a different way, e.g.

I can see what she was saying, why couldn't she see what I meant?

I can hear what she is saying, why couldn't she hear what I was saying?

Once you are able to recognise your own style, it opens up options to improve the way you think and communicate. Notice what happens when you flex your style.

MIND READING

Mind reading is where you make assumptions; add things in so that you can understand what is being said.

Here is a simple example:-

She always goes to yoga on Monday. The assumption is that she always does it and she always does it on a Monday, this of course may not be the case.

Here's another example:-

I know what he will say, because he always does that, when I ask him to put the bins out.

There will be times when you mind read and think you know what other people are thinking and why they do what they do.

Look back through your journal and find an example that you think is a mind read.

As you reread it, break it up, what predications did you make?

How can you rewrite it so that it is factual?

How does that make you feel?

CAUSE AND EFFECT

Some people believe that our internal emotional states (how we feel) are a direct effect of the actions of others or the effect of other external conditions such as the weather or the news on television and are never our fault or responsibility,

e.g.

See what you did, you made me so angry! How does what I'm doing cause you to choose to feel angry?

This awful weather is making me feel miserable. How does it make you feel miserable?

Because you didn't give me any feedback I will have to spend Sunday rereading the report and doing it all myself. Ask yourself, why didn't you ask for any feedback?

Nobody can make you feel anything, you make those choices yourself.

When you know this you can start to make changes. It is about acknowledging that the choices you make and how you feel belongs to you.

Go back to your journal entries and look for times where you have blamed others. Now rewrite them taking responsibility for them.

IS IT POSSIBLE?

Think of the words can, can't, have, haven't. Are you one of those people that always says – 'I can't do that because…' or 'I haven't got the time to do that'?

Find some journal examples where you have used the words can't and haven't. Ask:-

What if you could?

What if I did have?

Now rewrite those entries in the positive form.

PICTURE IT

Using art as therapy has become quite popular. One side is that simply doing something artistic is therapeutic and the other side is the analysis of what your art is saying to you. For me I love creating things for the fun of doing it without thinking too deeply about what it all means.

I can remember once being made redundant and feeling fed up. I took myself off on a course where I had to make my foot out of a lump of clay. The touch of the clay and the kneading was amazing for getting my thoughts focused, though the resulting foot was rather ugly and made me laugh, which lifted my spirits.

This is a really fun way of coming up with a solution to a problem or issue or even creating a plan.

Find an entry in your journal that you want to do something with.

Flick through some magazines or newspapers and start to pull out random pictures or words that appeal to you.

Get yourself a large sheet of paper; start to arrange the pictures and words so that they make some sense to you.

Now that you have your visual representation, start to write what these pictures and words mean to you and how they are helping to solve your problem or to create your plan.

THERE'S SOMETHING I WANT TO TELL YOU

Is there something you are reluctant to say to someone? We often hold our tongues and then wish that we had said something witty or clever later. Sometimes those conversations go around in our heads, driving us mad. Journaling is a great way to get them out and dealt with. Use this template to get you to the point where you can hold a sensible conversation where you say what you really want to say.

Situation – describe the situation, factually.

Tell – express what you want to say, what you want and what the consequences might be (nicely) if this doesn't happen.

Feedback – what advice would you give yourself?

Retell – express what you will say, specify what you want and what the consequences might be (nicely) if this doesn't happen How does that feel?

Keep doing this until you feel that what you want to say will work for you.

Write up the situation as if you were saying it in a more productive way, and practice with a friend or partner.

STRATEGIES

This exercise is looking at how we create our internal strategies. You may of course think that you just do things, however the more we reflect in our journal you will notice patterns to your behaviour.

Think of the last time you made a large, expensive purchase.

Walk yourself through the steps that you took to get to actually paying for it and bringing it home.

E.g. when I buy a computer I undertake lots of research but do not write any of my findings down. I read lots of reviews, go to the usual trusted places to buy to look at the specifications. I spend days discussing it with myself, going back to these web sites, trying to make absolutely sure that it's the right product with the right specification for my budget. I visit stores so that I can discuss it with another human to see if I have missed anything in my surmising and I touch the products. When I am completely satisfied with my internal reckoner, I buy from a site that I feel I can trust, which offers the quickest delivery at the best price.

In my example, although I haven't listed each of the steps you can see that I go through a process. To understand my strategy I would need to list every stage.

The next step is to go through each of your stages and, associate feelings, thoughts, emotions, sounds, smells etc. – you should end up with a list of each of the steps and the feelings that go with the steps.

E.g. the stage where I go to the shop to touch the product is very kinaesthetic, the texture is very important as is the way the keys respond to my fingers, do they bounce or what kind of pressure is needed? Etc..

Ask yourself, is this the same pattern you use when buying other things?

If not, plot your strategies for buying other things.

Once you feel comfortable with the process, consider your strategies for other areas of your life. How do you deal with interruptions or demands on your time, or being let down?

Go back through your journal, what patterns are you noticing?

Where can you interrupt the unhelpful patterns with new strategies. Reflect and write out new strategies, try them out, feedback to yourself and keep amending until you find a way that works for you.

LOOKING FOR OUTCOMES

To get the most out of any situation, you need to focus on the outcome (remember well formed outcomes) that you want to achieve. When we know what the outcome is, we can plan the journey.

Think of a problem or difficult situation that you have had.

Describe the situation - what did you see, feel, hear, who was with you, what did they say, what did you say, what did they do or not do, what did you do or not do?

Now answer the following questions:-

What was the other person's contribution towards that problem or situation?

What was your contribution?

How did both of you contribute to the problem?

What do you notice about the language you use?

What would you have liked to have happen instead?

How could you have reached your new desired outcome?

What could you do differently in the future?

What do you need to help you reach your outcome?

Will there be any consequences as a result of your new actions?

How will you know in the future that you are succeeding?

What will you do next time?

PERCEPTIONS

You cannot possibly know how or why somebody reacts to you in the way that they do. Everything that everybody does is clouded by their experience and the way that they filter information.

You may believe that you have said something in a certain way, in a particular tone and that you have been very clear in what you are trying to get across. Therefor it will shock you when they don't respond as expected. Because of course, what they are hearing and seeing was totally different to what you think you're projecting.

People see the world the way they are, not the way it is.

Looking back at a journal entry where there has been a miscommunication. What did you say or do and how did the other person react?

On a loose piece of paper write down what you really meant in full detail. Put it to one side.

Take a fresh sheet of paper and imagine that you are the other person. Write what you believe they observed during your interaction with them. What is important here is that you *imagine that you are them* and they are having a conversation or interaction with you.

When you have finished you have two sheets of paper in front of you; one about your perspective and one from their perspective.

You now have the opportunity to tell the other person how you feel about what recently happened.

YOU – tell the other person the situation from your perspective. IMAGINE YOU ARE THE OTHER PERSON – respond to you.

Put both of these sheets of paper down next to each other.

Now what I'd like you to do is to *imagine that you are a third person* who is looking at the information provided.

What advice do you have for both of these people?

How do you feel?

What new information springs to mind that you previously didn't see?

How will you choose to re-act or behave next time?

WISHES

A wish is a hope or desire for something. On our birthdays we blow out the candles and make three wishes. Or wish upon a star. No matter how fanciful you think making wishes are, it is actually a very useful and powerful way of taking your attention to a problem and looking for a solution.

Take something from your journal that you wish to solve or reflect upon.

If you could have 3 wishes that would solve your problem what would they be? They can be as fantastical as your like!

How does each of the wishes solve the problem?

How can you use this insight to solve this and other problems?

AROUND THE TABLE

We don't have to solve all of our problems all by ourselves, although sometimes it does feel like that. A great way to find solutions is to pretend that you have your own board of directors or team of amazing minds.

Get all of the best people around the table. Who are they, what qualities do they have and why have you chosen them?

Find a journal entry which is an issue you want to resolve.

Looking at the issue through the eyes of your expert team.

Ask each one in turn, using their skills and experience - what advice do they have for you?

Describe each of their perspectives.

Which answer(s) makes the most sense to you?

How can you now solve the problem?

ACTING AS IF IT WERE TRUE

Sometimes we are so bogged down with how we think things are that we can't see the wood for the trees. What we can do is re-look at the situation and try to imagine a different outcome.

We can act *as if* it were all ok and the problem has been solved or act as if we did really have that much confidence or creativity. Remember, we put our own barriers up and limits on ourselves.

Therefore, here's what we are going to do – trick our minds into to believing that we already can.

Think of a problem or a difficult situation that you have or had.

What led up to that situation, who played what role and what is the current state of play?

What is the ideal solution?

What needs to happen to make that true?

How would the situation change?

Rewrite the story as if it had a different ending.

EXAGGERATION AND DOWNPLAYING

Exaggeration and downplaying happens everywhere. Think of things you might say like 'I am dying for a drink' or 'I could kill for a beer', or 'Oh it was nothing really' or 'I would never do that'. Think of a company, who wants to sell you something, they will typically oversell the benefits, whilst a company who has done something wrong will minimise the impact.

Where else does this happen in your life?

Is it something you do?

When and why?

Think of a problem or a difficult situation that you have had.

Now exaggerate it so that it really is blown up out of proportion.

Then minimise it so it becomes a really trivial event.

Notice how you feel when the issue is either exaggerated or downplayed.

What do you learn?

How can you use this strategy again?

Where and when will you use this?

What have you learnt through the reflective writing exercises?

How can you use what you have learnt to start to make changes and heal your life?

Jacqui Malpass

Writing to Heal

REFLECTING THROUGH CREATIVE WRITING

"It took me fifteen years to discover I had no talent for writing, but I couldn't give it up because by that time I was too famous." Elizabeth Bishop

How can I turn journals into stories?

The final piece of Writing to Heal is to construct short stories from your journal entries. I have found that writing creative life stories, where I use events and people as inspiration, extremely cathartic. These stories put me in control and anything can happen.

This works because when you take something that you consider to be real (your current perception) and change the way in which you view it; it releases your attachments to the situation. With creative life writing you find ways to let go of your stuff, whilst also having fun.

Creative life writing is a pathway to self-discovery and transformation. Writing the stories of our past can help us consider how to have a healthy future. As we pour ourselves into words, we learn who we are, what has to change, where the opportunities to heal are, to grow and be able to tell a completely new story.

Use your journal for inspiration and weave these snippets, ideas, and revelations into your tales. You will have so much fun. I do.

Write about what you feel, not just what you know. In trying to find something that speaks to your own heart and soul, something you think is authentic, true, and compelling in the story you want to tell, others will want to read.

That is of course if you want to share. You may want to write your stories, just for you.

If you are writing to share, then the fundamental motive for writing your stories is to reveal the truth as you see it, to share your experiences and life. This brings honesty to your work. Shoot from the heart not the hip.

As you stand naked in front of your readers (and yourself), they will trust you and want to share your journey, although they may prefer to stay clothed.

For now, put pen to paper and trust that you will find your way to great stories, poems, and prose.

WHY STORIES?

Stories help to place us or the event in the big picture. As the story unfolds we can see patterns emerging, we can identify with our emotions, and we can find ways in which the story helps makes connections for us, so that we can make sense of our lives.

WHY YOUR STORY?

Imagine that your journal is going to be turned into a memoir or a novel. This is going to become the book of your life. You are in control, the storyline, characters and the ending belong to you and your imagination.

Every tale has a:-

Beginning, middle, and end.

Protagonist – you.

Other characters.

The thing that had to change - crisis.

The events leading up to the crisis.

The turning point.

How you got through the crisis.

The message you want to share.

And so does your journaling and storytelling.

LETS BEGIN TO WRITE YOUR STORY - YOUR BOOK

Let's carry on with the notion that we are writing a book about your life.

Title, what and who

Without thinking answer these questions

What is the title of the book about your life?

What would it be about, which slice of your life?

Who are you writing it for?

Looking back at the title and what it is about, what does that tell you about where you find yourself right now?

Next step in your story - Why do you want to tell?

There are many reasons for telling our stories, what is important is that you are clear about why YOU want to write it and what it will give you. Again, go with your imagination.

So why do you want to tell your story?

My mum wrote one of her books about her mum so that she could lay to rest some ghosts about her life and to make sense of her lack of grief for her mother's passing.

Which story?

Look back at the values you created for yourself, these are the values that underpin who you are and how you experience life. When you express your values through stories you not only have the power to move you, your stories will move others.

This is the story of you.

Now look at your *'where is my now'* exercise, this tells you what is going on right now, what your challenges and issues might be. Your timeline brings together everything that bought you here today.

This is the story of now.

What about the people in your life from the writing exercises chapter, who are they and how do you and they interact? What impact do they have on your life? What are the important relationships?

This is the story of your community.

Where these three stories overlap is a great place to start your storytelling.

Challenge, choice and outcome

Start sketching out your story with your challenge, what are your choices, and which outcome will you choose?

Challenge - What was your challenge? Why did you feel it was a challenge? It could be a challenge that you set yourself or a challenging situation.

Choices - Why did you make the choice you did? Choices are about our choices, not the ones you feel others forced on you, although that in itself is a choice.

Outcome - Why that outcome? What did you learn? What is the moral of your story? If someone reads your story, how would you want them to feel and to learn?

It's now up to you to go back through your journal and decide which of your 'stories' can be turned into poems, prose, short stories or maybe there really is a book in there? Trust the process and please put pen to paper and just write.

My best advice is to take any event or person, make something up, and have some fun. Laughter, they say is the best medicine.

Get into the right frame of mind.

Find the right writing space.

Let go of any fears that stop you believing that you can write.

Know that whatever comes out is perfect.

You can hone your first draft later, so just write.

Enjoy the process; let your unconscious mind guide you.

You may find that you are inspired to write a book (I hope so!).

THE STORY FRAMEWORK

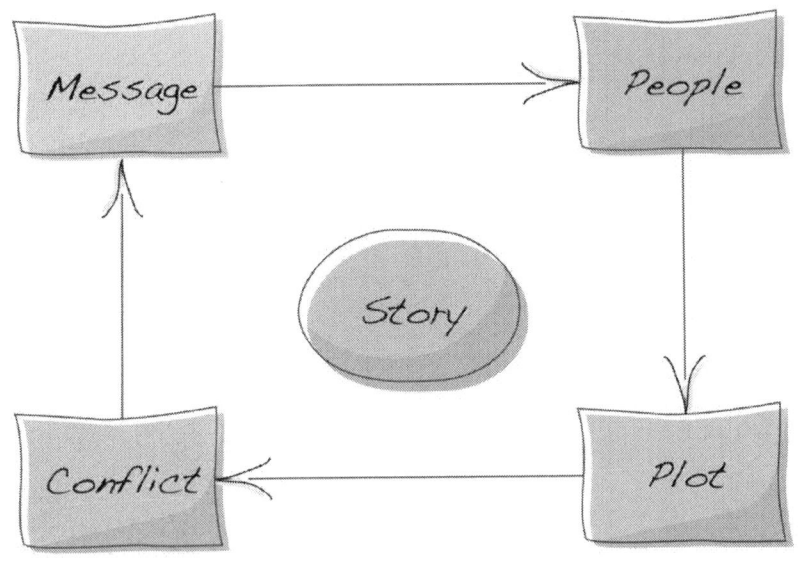

```
  Message ────────→ People
     ↑                 │
     │     Story       │
     │                 ↓
  Conflict ←────────  Plot
```

We are now going to use the story framework to bring it all together.

Writing to Heal

Creating characters (PEOPLE)

There is usually someone other than you at the heart of every story. In this exercise imagine that you are interviewing that person. We will use the information we glean to write a story about them.

Who is that person?

How old are they?

Male or female

Happy?

How would their friends describe them?

How would their enemies describe them?

Any children?

What do they do for a living?

What other career did they have?

What is the best thing that happened to them?

What is the worst thing that happened to them?

Are they political?

Is there anything they are passionate about?

Distinguishing features?

Educated?

What are they proudest of having achieved?

Any skeletons in the closet?

What food do they hate?

What last made them cry?

What is their story?

What are their values?

What is this character's relationship to the other people in the story?

Why is this person important?

How do they grow?

Now that you have a good feel for or idea about who they are, write a story about your person. If you need a prompt, use this picture to kick-start you.

The plot

The twists, turns, and encounters that take us from the first meeting to the final pages, where our main character's life is changed forever is the plot. We are left understanding why and how, then applying it to our lives and wondering what if.

Now are you creating a series of interconnected events, which flow seamlessly through the landscape of memory, carrying you over the rough bumps, steering you around the conflicts and on to triumph. How will the plot take us on a journey through your story?

Plot answers the basic questions of who, what, where, when, how, and why, making sense of the story's underlying meaning.

Writing to Heal

Who, what, why, when, where

We invariably write stories by pulling on our own experiences. We already know that by turning some of your journaling into a story you can begin to unpick it and rewrite it in a more positive way whilst having fun.

Choose you who, what, why, when and where. If you get stuck have a go at the following exercise to warn up your writing.

Write a story, by picking one thing from each of the sections, have some fun and just let your mind go free. Try to weave some of your experiences into it.

Where.......is your story going to start?

Airport - on your way to a trip of a lifetime.

In your favourite restaurant.

Paddington Station - under the announcement board.

Best friend's wedding reception.

A salsa class with a new handsome teacher.

When.....does it happen?

A winters evening in 2008.

Valentine's Day.

August 2107 – daytime.

Winter.

A dark November day.

New Year's Day, 2016.

3 a.m.

Who...is your protagonist?

> The lady with the all-over orange spray tan.
>
> A little old lady with a long blonde wig on.
>
> A woman running away from a violent husband.
>
> A short, balding man with a really tall girlfriend.
>
> A man who is cheating on his wife.

What....is the opening scenario?

> A set of keys have just fallen down a drain.
>
> The heel has just come off your shoe.
>
> A bag of money is sitting on the bus seat – take it and definitely get 2 years in jail, or just leave it.
>
> A lady's bag is snatched just after she got her pension.
>
> A stranger presses a key into your hand and then disappears into the crowd.
>
> Blocked drains.
>
> Someone finds a ringing mobile.
>
> A spilt drink.
>
> A letter asking you to call into a solicitor's office.

Why....is your character motivated to act? OR, what is the story's key emotion?

> Trust.
>
> Temptation.
>
> Running out of time.
>
> Jealousy.
>
> Self-doubt.
>
> Burning ambition.

Sorrow.

Revenge.

Pride.

Betrayal.

Conflict

Every story has a conflict. Him against her, you against the world, them against you and your internal emotions which are attached to your story. Whether you share or not. Your stories should move the reader (you or others) and tap into their emotional core. Emotions will pull your readers in faster than anything else and keep them wanting more. Emotions wind your readers in; they become involved with the story and identify with it. You will also be able to detach from your emotional attachment and move on.

Look for conflict, emotions, and passion in your story. The areas of your life which are conflicted are a great place to start. Examine why they are in conflict and what the steps are to resolving that conflict.

Remember that we don't just feel one emotion at a time, our emotions run into each other, often causing more confusion and stress. You are feeling these emotions for a reason.

Compare this…

I divorced my abusive husband and it was a bit of a bumpy ride. After he kept me hostage in our log cabin, I decided enough was enough.

To…

As his hands closed around my throat, I knew in that moment that I would rather be dead than spend another moment with him. It was like history repeating itself, I watched my mother cope with an alcoholic husband, but this was different, he held me captive for 3 months, not at home, but deep in the woods.

I didn't think I would ever feel the sun on my face again. He slipped up, the tables were turned, and I lived to tell you my story.

As you write to create emotional responses you will, as we have previously discussed evoke emotion in yourself. You will also be revealing so much more about you and your story. This is what makes it cathartic. Ask what is the moral of my story and what did I learn? How will others benefit from my writing?

Your conflict is the heart and soul of the story of you. It is the thing that sits beneath the story, the thing that rouses the emotion in others, the thing that has them wanting more, which enables them to discover more about you, your story and to identify with you.

What is your one word conflict?

Sum up your conflict in one to two sentences?

What makes it different?

What is the worst thing that could happen to you, our hero/heroine?

What is our hero/heroine's goal or outcome? Their reason for being? What stands in the way of the outcome?

What makes the hero/heroine interesting? Not likeable, interesting?

What is your hero/heroine's best quality? And the opposite of that?

How does the hero/heroine change and overcome their conflict?

Does the story start and end in the right place? Where should it start and end?

How are you propelling the story along? Can you set it off in one direction and then suddenly twist it, creating a 'blimey I wasn't expecting that' moment? What are those different directions?

Is there something that could emerge from the story, which also gives it a twist that we weren't expecting?

What is the other side of your story?

Go back to the previous section and look at the:-

Why….is your character motivated to act? OR, what is the story's key emotion?

Rewrite any part of your story substituting emotions and conflicts that are rearing their ugly head in your life. Bring them to the fore and look at how you can rewrite them.

Message or moral

What is the moral of your story? What is the key message that you and your reader must take away? What is the lesson that you learn from this book of your life? What will you do as a result of discovering the moral of your story?

Looking at any of your journals and stories and reflect on what you think the key message is. Is it what you expected?

Your book

Using the story framework and your journal, write some stories as long or as short as you want. They are amazing for reflection, healing and growth. And as I said, please do have some fun.

METAPHOR

All of us speak, write and think in metaphors every day. They can't be avoided; metaphors are built into our language.

Metaphor is an implied comparison which is made between two unlike things that have something in common. The word metaphor comes from a Greek word meaning to "transfer" or "carry across." Metaphors "carry" meaning from one word, image, or idea to another.

Life is the journey, not the destination.

If I were to ask you to describe how you felt right now you might say *I feel as if I have been through the mill.*

If I asked about a relationship you may say, *my heart was broken.*

Other metaphors

I am in pieces. / I am torn up.

I am a ship out to sea.

I am on a journey.

Wounds heal with time.

Just keep swimming against the tide.

I am being eaten up.

Life is the journey, not the destination.

When you are struggling to give meaning to a feeling or personal experience metaphor can help you to make sense of things and to make meaning. They also allow us to really understand what is going on.

The mind makes connections, sees things as patterns, this includes our language. There is a link between the mind and the disease that our bodies express.

In healing, the link that we can use to examine the body through the mind is metaphor. This works because we are storytelling creatures and everything in our lives is part of our story.

With our physical symptoms our mind is telling a specific story.

This is the story of our body.

Metaphor bypasses conscious thought and speaks directly to the unconscious mind. What we need to do is to interpret what this means to us.

Ask yourself today – what metaphor describes how you feel? Is it part of:

Story of you?

Story of your now?

Story of your community?

Story of your body?

Pick a metaphor, write a story and ask:-

What does it mean?

What can you see, feel, hear? Describe everything.

Change the image through your words.

By understanding and making meaning from the story that you are writing you can find the underlying issues, problems and unhelpful thought processes. This is how the use of metaphor gives us insight into healing ourselves.

Q AND A

Imagine that you are famous, answer these questions:

What did you learn from your parents?

When you were 13, what did you want to be when you grew up?

If you could give your childhood self some advice, what would it be?

What's your biggest fear?

When was the last time you cried?

Which book changed your life?

What is your guilty pleasure?

Are you an optimist or a pessimist? Why?

Who do you listen to when you need critical advice?

Do you ever have a crisis of confidence?

Now write a story about the person you have just described, they have just won an opportunity to star in a TV show, but it's on the same day that they have to be at a friend's wedding. What happens?

A PLACE IN TIME

Pick a journal entry that you want to explore. You have 10 minutes to draw your place in time. No artistic skill needed!

Pick a starting point in the story; it could be your home, school, work.

Writing to Heal

Draw the journey to the end point, which might be work, the library, a favourite park, a friend's house or a future goal.

Scribble on the map add anything that you experience, see, feel or hear on the way.

Now write a story about the journey. How did you get from A to B? Who did you meet on the way? What did they say? Did you eat or drink anything? What were you wearing? Etc.

PERSPECTIVES

Perspective or point of view is how the storyteller views what is happening and therefore shapes how they portray what they have seen to the reader.

First person narrative means writing from the "I" point of view. As in: I walked down the street, turning around, I looked at the dog following me.

Third person narrative form is writing from the he/she point of view. As in - She walked down the street, turning around to look at the dog that was following her.

Write a story about someone (real or fictional) who may be irritating you, or there's something about their manner that bugs you, they may have offended you or you can't get on with them, but would like to.

Invent someone really nasty and have some fun.

Write it in the third person, e.g.

Miranda pushed herself to the front of the restaurant queue as usual. She was one of those really pushy women who always thought she had some kind of right, to have the best of everything. Today she was dressed like a footballer's wife, clanking her expensive jewellery for all to see.

Write the same story as if you were that person.

Write it in the first person, e.g.

I arrived at the restaurant late for a meeting that was make or break for my marriage. I had found out 2 months ago that my husband was cheating on me and despite not wanting to stay and being torn apart by this revelation I knew I loved him and wanted to work it out. He said I was always too busy building my business and had no time for him.

THROUGH THE LOOKING GLASS

Sometimes we really don't see what others see. You may be told you look fantastic, yet the person you see in the mirror, or photo looks old and fat. This is simply our perspective and negative feelings getting in the way of reality.

Get a recent photograph of yourself. Place the photograph in front of you. Now answer these questions.

Looking at that person, and stand back from the fact that it is you.

What do you see, what are you wearing, what colours do you have on, what is the style of your clothing, are you dressed for business or leisure, what is your hairstyle like, your facial expression, who else is in the picture with you.

Now imagine that you have never met yourself. What do you learn about the person in the picture?

Write a story about the person in the picture. You can make up anything that you like. Perhaps it's the first day of a new job, or they have just been made redundant and decide to buy a camper van and go traveling for 3 months.

THE STRANGER

We can often learn a lot about ourselves from looking through others' eyes. The key is to get inside the stranger's skin, become them, watching you.

Write a short story about what the stranger saw.

A stranger observes something that you did.

Describe the stranger and try to imagine what that stranger thinks about your activities. Perhaps you are having a conversation?

In writing the story, what have you learned about the stranger and what have you learned about yourself?

ON YOUR SIDE OF THE STREET

Read 'Other side of the street' and ask yourself which side of the street are you on and what has to happen to move you to the sunny side of the street?

Bring to mind someone you know who is very negative and you as the happy positive person you know you are. Write a poem about your two sides of the street.

Which side of the street are you on?

Jacqui Malpass

Other side of the street

Awaking to the sound of the birds singing, you think 'bugger off'.

You walk by the running river and see only the concrete path

Overhead the emerging skies are filled with hope, you see rain

Through your window the blossoms are wilting, leaves turning brown

The tea has no taste; it's a hot, wet morning drink

Toast like cardboard, salty greasy butter, jam sickly and sweet

You hate today, it's like every other day, nobody cares, and you know it

Hiding from the knock on the door, nobody calls for you

You get through life, nothing to look forward to, frequent hot, violent tears

Meanwhile on the other side of the street

The curtains are open, the daylight streams in, a new day begins

You awake with weak warm sun on your face, cocooned in your duvet, safe

The chorus greets you, nature's daily miracle sings to you

Looking out of your window, the outside calls for your company

Light perfumed tea, delicate on your palette, lingers in your mouth

Alive today and every day, living in the now, freedom, you can touch it

Later when walking by the sea, thundering sounds stir your soul

Conversation and laughter with friends, white wine, black beer, and chocolate

Kisses and gentle touches from your lover to come

You seize the day, nothing to be feared, and everything to be savoured and learned

Meanwhile on the other side of the street

VISUALISATION

"Imagination is more important than knowledge." Albert Einstein

The real key to turning imagination into reality is acting *as if* (which you should have already tried) the imagined scene were real and already accomplished. Instead of pretending it is a scene from the future, imagine it as though you are truly experiencing it in the present. Thinking is doing and thoughts become our reality.

Henry Ford, founder of the Ford Motor Company said:

"There are people who think they can, and people who think they can't and both are right!"

Take anything about your life that you would like to heal, change or enhance.

> Sit back, relax, close your eyes, and think about the outcome - what you would really like to happen next time or how you would like a future event to go.
>
> Don't put any limitations on it, and don't shroud it with doubt. Remember, there is no one who is going to judge this fantasy and no one who is going to prevent it from happening.
>
> Only you have the power to deter its realisation. You have the power to do anything you want, if you first imagine it in your mind's eye.
>
> Once you have the picture in your mind, make it bigger, brighter, and more colourful, bring it closer to you.
>
> Keep doing this until it feels so real you can actually touch it.

Record what you see, hear, and feel.

What else can you take a note of?

Visualisation by its very nature is visual; to make this more real, add in your other senses. This will make it more powerful.

Consider this. When you don't know how, you usually go find someone who does. What if that doesn't work and no one knows? How about you just do something that just moves you in the right direction – the one you have just visualised.

Holding what you have just visualised in your minds eye, write a short story about it.

You could also write a story about your perfect day. Where are you, what are you doing, who are you with and what makes it a perfect day?

WANT TO LEARN MORE ABOUT CREATIVE WRITING?

There are many books on how to write creatively and my recommendation is that you explore these if you want more guidance. Additionally, attend creative writing classes, where you will learn your craft amongst other passionate writers and you will gain constructive feedback on your work.

> What stories will you write?
> Who will feature in your stories?
> What happens to the people you write about?
> What are the themes for your stories?
> Will you turn your stories into a book?

TELLING TALES

"How vain it is to sit down to write when you have not stood up to live." Henry David Thoreau, Journal, 19 August 1851

Sharing short stories

JOURNAL EXCERPTS AND STORIES

In this chapter, I share with you some of my writing adventures, because to me, this is what they have been. I adore writing, seeing links, being creative, changing my mind-set, and exploring new ways to tackle old stuff.

THE VOICE

From the journal

Day 1

The desk is ready, I have sorted out her computer, it will be great to have a new s development manager to work along-side me. They tell me she has been in sales for years and is a real go getter.

End of week 1

It's only been a week, I am not sure if I can stand working with this person. I caught the boys laughing behind her back every time she touches me. They have started to ask what I will be wearing to work just in case she decides to comment. She must be colour blind, because this week she told me my grey suit was a better shade of brown for me. And if she calls me "Oi missus" again I will head butt her.

Week 2

The boys have decided that her name should be Edward because she looks like a man and has man's hands and an Adam's apple – she doesn't, but that's beside the point. I tell them that it's not nice but laugh anyway. They tell me they don't like her.

If she asks me one more time how to use Outlook I swear I will brain her. And can someone turn off the Clash should I stay or should I go that she plays endlessly – the answer is go.

Her voice does my head in and I have asked her again to stop calling me missus, she thinks its funny – we'll see. I am being driven mad.

Week 3

Wednesday and I have the answer, I am at home. I finish a call with her and I am so mad. I put her name on a piece of paper and jump on it. Then I burn it. It feels good and at least no one can see me. I tell the boys they laugh. Edward has stuck; the whole office calls her that now.

Week 4

I can't take anymore. I came in at 7am and moved my desk as far away from her as possible. She was quite rude about it, shame. I lost my temper when she told me I couldn't move without her permission. As I was screaming at her I could see the boys laughing. Little buggers they get away with it, because she thinks I am the one being nasty. Ho hum, she won't be telling me what to do in a hurry again.

I went to HR and explained about her behaviour and how she was being rude to not only me but to my team and how I had tried to talk to her. They said to try and keep it nice. At least they noted it all down and I wasn't the only one who had been in.

Speak too soon. She's back on to me. This time, I took her outside for a walk and a chat. Those boys they are laughing again. I will kill them too.

There's been a bet on for when she will leave; I now dislike her so much I put a fiver on for March.

Story - The voice

The voice belongs to a 50 something bimbette. Blond hair threatened into place, frames the face with gold clad bulging eyes and pink lipsticked mouth, out of which comes the ceaseless noise. I wonder why it never stops, endless mumbles which get louder when it wants us to snap to attention.

I always tell the voice I wasn't aware that it was addressing me, so that I don't have to be drawn into its shapeless world. The voice troubles me, I can't place its owner who lives in Bristol but doesn't have that West Country twang. There's a falseness, its hiding its origins, I know because, because is becoorse.

I learn to hate the voice, it criticises my clothes, tucks me in and its hands touch my body uninvited. It's only been sending shrill messages for a week and I already need to escape. The pink hole is open more than it is shut and after a short while I move my desk to the other side of the room, for some much needed peace. The voice mutters under its breath only to rise to a nasty hiss when it demands 'how dare I move'. It snarls and threatens me. It's too late I lose my temper; its snotty falseness grates me.

Writing to Heal

The voice has landed on a nerve and jars me; the code imprinted on the ganglia, bullets in place the voice pulls the trigger. I can never hear it again without bile rising.

It's another day, I am deliberately ignoring it. It rises higher lamenting the journey to work, no one is listening, the monkey screeches louder as if to declare 'you will listen to me'. We all, my colleagues and I continue to tap tap on our computers; no one lifts their eyes, for to catch its eye will give it life. It stops, silence, but the lingering echo wraps itself around each of us, rubbing harsh salt into our ears. I daren't look up, until the extra tap tap of its keyboard is added to ours.

Eventually my bladder betrays me and I try to sneak across the uncarpeted room, past its desk. No chance. 'Oi missus'. The pink circled hole opens and the brittle irritating false notes clatter out. The commentary on the inadequacy of the last person it had barked at flies over my head. I rush by and out of the door. Silence. The temptation not to return is great and I linger by the coffee machine, take a deep breath and eventually head back, I fly through the door and straight to my desk. Tap tap.

We place bets on when will the voice leave, it has only been with us a few months. I write its name on a piece paper and stamp on it, then burn it gleefully hoping that my magic incantation will bring the leaving date closer. No such luck. In the office the voice speaks differently to the men it wants to manipulate, its light and fluffy, it tinkles girlishly and coo coo's like a dove. To the women who its thinks are beneath it, it is harsh and wintery, sharp like broken glass as it cuts you with its demands. To the women it perceives as equal it rallies along with jokey anecdotes and giggles sympathetically to their problems and plight. People complain about the voice, it is shocked and sniffles to show that it has feeling. No one cares, too late the damage is done, and the voice must leave.

BECCIS HOLIDAY
From the journal
Wednesday

There goes the doorbell again, I've told Ben my lodger not to answer the door, but too late he is there and she is in, telling me all about her awful day and how everyone picks on her. I opened another bottle of wine and helped her drown her sorrows. This is the third time this week and it's only Wednesday.

Sunday

I tried not to laugh as Ben bit into the tea towel to stop himself laughing. She had just finished telling us that she had been in the bath all day, exfoliating, shaving, scrubbing, face pack and moisturising, it had taken 4 hours to get her skin this soft and now she had her arm out for me to stroke. Every time she has a new man we go through this. And she made a comment again that I should spend more time on myself and eat a bit more as I was looking too thin and shapeless. That hurt. I will add that to the list of other careless things she has said. I wonder sometimes why I have her as a friend. A lesser person's confidence would be shattered. I think she must mean well, so I will ignore her.

Friday

I got a text to say that the bank has approved her loan to do up the house and did I want to come shopping. I declined.

Saturday

I went over for tea as arranged. She was flustered and excited. Her new clothes were hanging up, leather jacket, 2 pairs of trousers, a jumper, 3 pairs of shoes and 2 handbags. They were lovely, she does have great taste. You have to laugh she only spent £1500. So that's only £28.5k left to do the house. After a few glasses of wine I decide to come home, I wanted a quiet night.

Two weeks later

She was back around again crying. More wine and I fed her half my dinner. She seems to know just when I am going to eat. She was rabbiting on about the latest man and her new car. I am so tired of all of this. Even so I have somehow agreed to go on holiday with her. How will that work I am an early bird and I hate the beach?

Story - Beccis holiday

Admiring herself in the mirror Becci waited anxiously for the call. For 3 hours she had been exfoliating, moisturising, preening, and pampering. Glancing at her new Tag, a recent present to herself, she wondered where he could be.

She'd met him 2 days ago when she'd stumbled on the cobbles outside the cathedral. The heel from her new Jimmy Choo shoes had come off and as the hot wet tears fell onto her French polished toe nails, a crisp white handkerchief appeared and proceeded to mop up the dark streaks of mascara running down her carefully made up face.

She glanced up, not her normal type, too hairy and not well dressed; she smiled her award winning smile she normally reserved for her targets. Picking up her heel, he laughed and passing it to her he declared in his very English accent, we must get you some sensible shoes. He grabbed her hand and dragged her off to Conti's, her favourite Vienna café, ordered her a Cappuccino and saccher cake before she could argue. The stranger became Marcus and invited her to dine that evening, with nothing better to do she agreed.

She had been waiting for Marcus wearing her new black linen suit, with red bra top and high red sling backs when the hand reached along the bar, his touch electrifying her and while gazing deep into her eyes asked casually if she would like a drink.

This man was instinctively the kind of man she went for, dark, smooth, and expensively dressed, chest hairs peeking through the open necked shirt. His trousers showed off his taught buttocks and draped over his beautifully cleaned shoes. Everything about him cried fuck me.

The manicured hands teasingly pulled her close to him, she could hear her heart beating, the blood rushing in her ears, her ovaries popped, she was lost and didn't care.

Barely through the door of his room, clothes discarded, their hot fierce kisses fell into an all night release of lust.

Teasing her blonde straight hair into place, she felt only slightly ashamed as she texted Marcus to apologise for not meeting him. He replied there was always the following night and she had agreed.

She slung her Burberry over her slender bare bronzed shoulder, musing that she should really stop spending the house renovation money; she had whittled her £30k to £10k in just 2 short months. Still she thought £10k could still go a long way to making her aunt's house liveable.

Heading out to meet Marcus, she stopped at the cash point to discover her card was missing. In a panic she called the bank to cancel the card and was shocked to be told that her account was now in arrears.

Marcus meanwhile was enjoying his first decent meal in 3 months since losing his job.

GRANDDADS TREE

From the journal

That was a weird night. Mum and I were talking as usual, I had a glass of cold white wine in one hand and the other on dad, for some reason he was freaking me and I had to keep checking that he was breathing. He was, but he didn't look right. Silly man why did he have to destroy his body with all that drinking? My dad died 15th March, 2012 at 17.20pm; I was with him, holding his hand. This is for dad.

Story - Granddads tree

We visited granddads house every summer, always the week just before going back to school. Granddad played draughts with me, he called them chequers and cackled when he won, which he always did. Every year he told me the same story about the man in Palestine and the gun, right after his victory, 'it was him or me'. I never understood and defeated I retreated to the gardens behind the house. The garden was full of trees; there was one, that reminded me of Parma violets.

Dad told me that granddads dad had planted the trees and that one was very special. He chose it for my great grandmother and he had carved their initials in the bark just before proposing to her. Dad said that granddad had done the same. It was my tree. There were only ever 2 lots of initials and I wondered why my mum and dads weren't there.

The discovery of a hidey hole soon made me forget. Every year I left a little treasure that I had found for the fairy that lived amongst the leaves. Some years it was joined by something from someone else, I am not sure who, but I think it was granddad; there was just something in his eye.

One summer I was hiding in the tree, dozing as you do when tired from your adventures, when I heard them. Divorce, that's all I heard that summer. I wasn't sure what it was, but it looked and sounded serious. I didn't dare move a muscle, but made a pledge to leave a note to the tree fairy to make sure that mum and dad were kinder to each other. It must have worked, because they stayed together.

Over the years their fights became bickers, dampened by the heat of Spain's summers. They moved to Spain for a new life. Dad's new life ravaged his body, and now he slept almost all day.

Last autumn I decided on a last minute holiday and arrived to find him asleep as usual on the sofa, muttering, take me to the tree. Mum just tutted and looked that way, that said it all.

Glass of wine in one hand, my other on him, mum and I caught up.

Three weeks later I am back at the tree. Dad is with me. I put him in the hole and ask the tree fairy to take him safely home.

It is only then I notice their initials, PD and GM.

Jacqui Malpass

Writing to Heal

OTHER STORIES, POEMS & PROSE

"If you can tell stories, create characters, devise incidents, and have sincerity and passion, it doesn't matter a damn how you write." Somerset Maugham

TOMORROW

If I were to die tomorrow
Who could make another me?
Not I, for I will be gone
Nor you, for you do not know
the me, that lives, breathes and exists.

You know what you can see
or hear, touch and smell
But not that, that is
the stuff that dwells, in here
when I am alone, with me.

What do you know
or think you know?
What bits will you add
to make me
the way that you
wanted to see me?
So that I fit into
your world.

That world that I didn't see
or touch, hear or smell
That's your place to dwell
Not mine, nor me.

And left as a seed
How would you grow
the new me?

WHAT IF YOU NEVER EXISTED?

What if, you, when gone, never existed

Just born, married and died, simply listed

No record or clue, nothing to say

What you did or how you loved, nowt, not a clue

Only a line in some musty book or digital record

That didn't show how you'd lived, by the sword

What if, your life was laughter and fun

And every day you looked for the sun

Watched it rise and fall, making the most of every day

And in each and every moment, you thought of something to say

That would make a difference, but then

You never did, who cared what you did, when?

What if, you'd come through hell and back again

Been beaten, black and blue and lived in pain

Or mothered a child, who died too young

Lost your god and words of love, never left your tongue

If all you had to show, were ten photos and a few quid

What a shame, that you didn't tell us what you did

LEAVING HOME

Standing back from the road, I can see my home, tendrils of ivy skulk over rotten windows, embrace solid grey stones, overhead the empty attic window stares uncaringly.

Cold chill, sepia autumn light, highlights leaves fading from green to gold falling silently to adorn the frozen grass.

The front door, blue-grey, dirty from the endless stream of cars which pass it by, adds to the melancholy.

It opens to my home, exposing the warm colours, inviting. Lingering smell of times gone by, now masked by scented candles.

Can you hear the silence and feel the peace?

Disturbed only by the whir of the computer and tapping of keys, communicating with a digital world.

Gazing out of the window I can see the rambling garden, filled with remnants of the life I once lived.

Escaping from my other life, this, is the place where friends and I come to hide and to seek solace, to sip a chilled white wine, to chatter.

I have loved it here, I disengage, let go, pass it on, fill with memories, my home, only bricks and mortar, to a future which lies elsewhere.

GREEN DRESS

For 5 years green dress and I were best friends, she was short, straight, soft and silent, you couldn't really ask for much more in a friend. She clung to me on nights out, laughed at my jokes, helped me get dates, and danced like a demon, there wasn't much she couldn't do.

Hidden under a dark green sweat shirt she came with me to mums quiz night, all was ok until the dancing began and my father dragged her onto the dance floor, he insisted she throw off the ugly jumper and come out to play. It was only then that she let me down, there peaking through the straps on my bare shoulder, the trident and tail of a new and glistening large devil tattoo.

Dad called me common, green dress said sod him its your body, I believed her. 3 weeks later she came with me to Monaco, hot nights in expensive bars was much more her thing. Dark Italians touching her, wanting her.

One short brooding type sucked my finger and proclaimed love, she had other ideas and whisked my out of the dimly lit room, helped me quickly up the stairs out into the balmy night.

On our return we sadly fell out for a short while, a forgotten exercise routine and a few too many boozy nights out squeezed her out of my life. I didn't forget her and when sometime after I left the note 'please leave immediately' on the microwave to the maniac man called husband, she reminded me that we should forget about the fat, renew our friendship and try again. In 3 short months we were back at it again enjoying ourselves and our new found freedom.

Which brings me to the last night we partied together. In the week leading up to that night in Cardiff, she lay there on the bed encouraging me to wax and tan my legs, suggesting that curls would look sexy, not forgetting full war paint and high patent black court shoes. That last night we strutted our stuff on the dance floor watched by the soon to be ex husband, he'd had his chance she reminded me. She bought me home safe and sound that night like she always did, this time to the new man in my life. He for his part didn't know how close our friendship was, so every night he wined and dined me and sadly green dress was once again left to hang around by herself, devoted to the end.

In a safe plastic bag, green dress stayed hidden for over 15 years. A few weeks ago she called out my name, there she was just the same, sexy sassy and my mate. My body no longer that of a 30 something looks longingly at green dress. She coaxes me, come on, put me on, you need some fun. Look at your legs she cries, get them out show the others how its done. I wiggled and squeeze, she just fits, it's a sign.

BELLA AND THE EGG

Bella pulled her tired body from the bed, leaving behind the rank odour emanating from her husband. Wrapping the drab snagged pale blue candlewick dressing gown around her she shuffled quietly downstairs to the kitchen. Sixteen steps. She lifted the waiting pan and filled it exactly to the etched line, added just one egg, one cap of cider vinegar and lit the burner. With the timer set she flicked on the kettle, surveyed the worktop, cup, teabag, sugar, milk, plate, spoons, all perfectly positioned. She headed to the table, four steps.

Bella smiled, today was going to be a good day. Her eyes surveyed her kitchen, pristine. Yesterday Bella had worked all day, making the house look like a new pin, not a thing out of place, no dust, plumped cushions correctly aligned, fresh bed linen smoothed, clean towels folded, spotless kitchen, sparkling toilets, a show house, flawless.

This was her home, she had acquired it when her first husband of only 5 years had sadly passed away, and he had been the love of her life. Husband number two, his friend, had appeared to help her through the pain; he stayed and persuaded the numbed Bella to marry him. She gave up her career and had looked after him ever since.

The ting of the timer bought her back to the present. The egg was ready, washed under cold water, dried and placed in its holder, partnered with thick buttered bread, sweet builder's tea and today a fresh homemade lemon muffin. The egg was perfect, the chickens had been laying well since their arrival last summer, she used one egg for his breakfast and one for the four muffins.

Pulling fresh latex gloves over her sore cracked hands Bella completed her breakfast routine in time for the arrival of her husband at exactly 7.04. In his usual greedy style he gobbled his food and on discovering the extra treat wolfed that too. He burped and looked up in exasperation as Bella handed him her bottle of sleeping pills to be opened.

As he showered and dressed for today's meeting, 2 hours' drive away, she organised his lunch, sandwiches, crisps and 2 more muffins. She placed the packed food by the front door. Fourteen steps. At 8.27 he shut the door and was gone. Bella cleaned the kitchen, bleaching all of the surfaces, just as she did every morning.

Back in the bedroom. Thirty steps. Bella opened the drawer of the bedside cabinet checking the contents. Pleased that all was in order, she changed the bed, collected all of the towels, yesterday's clothes and pyjamas and placed them all in the washing basket ready for a hot wash.

In the bathroom Bella prepared for her bath. She placed cool lavender oil into the water and candles by the side of the bath, along with an old pink towel. She counted the rings created from the last drips, fifteen. Bathed, soothed wrapped in her old dressing gown, with everything as it should be Bella headed to the sofa. Seventeen steps.

Sometime later Bella was roused from her peaceful sleep to find 2 policemen at her door. Her husband, they explained, had lost control of his car and careered headlong into an oncoming lorry, they were, they said sorry for her loss. They held onto Bella as her legs gave way and led her easily to the kitchen where they sat her down, made her tea, explained exactly what had happened and what was to come.

When they had gone Bella headed back upstairs, opened the wardrobe, caressing a smart black suit as she reached for a neatly folded soft fluffy pink dressing gown. She walked slowly back to the bathroom. Bella knelt by her bath, put in the plug, sniffed then dropped in a Jo Malone bath oil, turned on the taps, watching as the oils formed small islands of heaven against the rushing water. Standing to remove her old dressing gown and placing it in the waiting bin liner, Bella caught her flesh in the mirror; she stopped, stared at the bruised and battered body. Smiling, that too would soon be gone.

RESOURCES

For more information, hints, tips, workshops, etc. please visit:-

www.jacquimalpass.com

If you are inspired and want to write a book, I work as a book coach and specialise in memoir / life story and business books.

My style is intuitive and we collaborate to find the heart and soul of your book, get it planned, written, published and sold.

You can contact me by email jacqui@jacquimalpass.com.

YOUTUBE

Head over to YouTube where there are lots of videos and resources on writing. http://www.youtube.com/user/jacquimalpass/videos

FACEBOOK

https://www.facebook.com/TheWordAlchemist

https://www.facebook.com/groups/thebigbookchallenge

PENNEBAKER RESEARCH

Pennebaker, James W. "Writing about Emotional Experiences as a Therapeutic Process." Psychological Science 8.3 (May 1997): 162-166.

http://homepage.psy.utexas.edu/homepage/faculty/Pennebaker/Reprints/P1997.pdf

ONLINE COURSES

Writing to Heal - http://www.udemy.com/writing-to-heal/ Use coupon code WTHB01 to access this course at a discount.

BOOKS THAT INSPIRE ME

The Magic - Rhonda Byrne

This is the most recent book on journaling that I have read and I highly recommend it.

"In The Magic a great mystery from a sacred text is revealed, and with this knowledge Rhonda Byrne takes the reader on a life-changing journey for 28 days. Step by step, day-by-day, secret teachings, revelations, and scientific law are brought together to form 28 simple practices that open the reader's eyes to a new world, and lead them to a dream life."

www.amazon.co.uk

PHOTOS AND ILLUSTRATIONS

© auryndrikson - Fotolia.com

iStockPhoto

Jacqui Malpass

ABOUT THE AUTHOR

Jacqui started writing at a young age. Prose, poetry, creative writing. She has always kept journals and written, not thinking that anyone would want to read it. However, three years ago, she decided that her mission was to help people tell their stories and turn them into published books. She left a highly successful marketing career and now works with people just like you to discover book ideas, write and get published.

Jacqui is an expert at getting your story out, and really finding the essence of what you want to say. And then saying it so that it is engaging and makes someone want to pick up and read your book.

.Jacqui believes that writing heals and indeed many of her clients come to her to write business books, only to discover that there are elements of their life meandering through the themes, that need clarity and she works to help them overcome any stumbling blocks and find a way to heal these through their writing or via other means.

Jacqui created Million Stories Project to inspire, motivate, and support anyone who wants to get their life story written. The project enables people to share their short life stories and she turns these into anthologies to support not for profit organisations by donating funds raised from the sales of the books. Her dream is to create a creative village in Spain, where aspiring writers from all over the world can come together for affordable writing holidays and breaks.

Outside of writing and coaching you can find her walking her beautiful dog Ferdy, taking yoga classes, and swimming.

FREEBIES

Each of my books has been through the proofing and editing process. With the best will in the world, errors happen. To this end I would like to offer you a deal. If you find an error, email me and tell me what it is and where it is. Plus……

Tell me three ways in which this book can be improved.

Email me at jacqui@jacquimalpass.com

I will send you the updated version of this book (as a PDF or Kindle) and one of my other books free of charge (as a PDF or Kindle).

I am blessed that you are reading this and I will be delighted to hear that you have made good use of the book, are getting your stuff out, and taking small steps towards the life and understanding that you want and deserve, as well as some great stories.

ENDS

Printed in Poland
by Amazon Fulfillment
Poland Sp. z o.o., Wrocław